PHYSICIAN ASSISTANT SCHOOL INTERVIEW GUIDE

TIPS, TRICKS, AND TECHNIQUES TO IMPRESS YOUR INTERVIEWERS

SAVANNA PERRY, PA-C

Physician Assistant School Interview Guide

Copyright © 2018 by Savanna Perry

1st Edition.

Instagram: @thePAplatform

Twitter: @thePAplatform

Facebook: @thePAplatform

ISBN 13: 978-1-7320760-0-6

ISBN-10: 1-7320760-0-6

Published by The PA Platform, LLC through Kindle Direct Publishing.

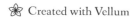 Created with Vellum

Lane - My biggest fan and supporter. You're the best <3

Dad - Thanks for always pushing me to do more than I think I can. And telling me about PAs.

Mom - You put almost as much work into this as I did. Love you and I owe you lunch.

GET SOME FREE STUFF!

To thank you for purchasing my book, I want to give you a **free** download of the Interview Preparation Worksheets from Chapter 13 and the Mock Interview Guide from Chapter 14! Visit the link below to get yours now!

---

http://www.thepaplatform.com/freeguide

ABOUT THE AUTHOR

Savanna Perry, PA-C graduated from Augusta University's Physician Assistant Program in 2014. As a new grad, she created The PA Platform, a website to assist students in becoming physician assistants. After helping hundreds of students gain acceptance through mock interviews, Savanna is sharing her advice in this book. She currently practices full time in outpatient dermatology. Savanna is also the creator of The Pre-PA Club podcast.

For more information:
www.thePAplatform.com
savanna@thepaplatform.com

instagram.com/thePAplatform
facebook.com/thePAplatform
twitter.com/thePAplatform

TABLE OF CONTENTS

FOREWORD

What do Physician Assistant programs look for in applicants? How can you set yourself apart from your peers? How can you exude more confidence when asked about your personal journey to become a PA?

There is plenty of material out there to help pre-Physician Assistant students prepare for interview day, but so much of it is outdated, transcribed based on the memory of clinicians that graduated years ago. There hasn't been a reliable, updated resource for students interested in a career as a Physician Assistant. Until now.

After I founded myPAresource, I searched to find someone who shared the same passion- helping spread the word about the PA profession and the importance of our role within the community. From the first time I spoke with Savanna I knew she was someone who loved coaching future PA students through the application process. Both of us remembered where we started: clueless postgrads with a passion for helping others. We both searched for reliable resources that could tell us what to expect on our journey to become Physician Assistants. Back then, neither of us were confident during our interviews about our abilities as future PA students, and we even responded to seemingly simple questions with notably embarrassing responses. Frankly, I'm surprised they accepted either of us. But the more we sat in on interviews at our respective PA programs, the more we became familiar with what it was that admissions panels looked for in their prospective students. And once Savanna realized that many applicants could benefit from these experiences, she took it upon herself to help guide future PAs through the process.

I've had the pleasure of working with Savanna Perry, PA-C, for the past few years as she acted as a true mentor for those interested in serving others in the roll of a Physician Assistant. It's rare to find someone, even in healthcare, as interested in helping others as Savanna. In addition to exuding passion every day in her clinic, she also radiates excitement and joy when given the opportunity to mentor others and help them along their journey to become a PA. Since graduating, she has not only improved the lives of her patients, but also boosted the confidence and knowledge of her mentees regarding the application process and what to expect moving forward. She's taken what she's learned from personal experience and consolidated her tips and tricks to help applicants perform better when it matters most.

This book will help you look within yourself and realize that you can (and will) stand out during your PA school interview. Savanna has sat on admissions panels and interviewed countless pre-PA applicants. She knows what admissions committees look for in their prospective students and will help you set yourself apart on one of the most important days of your life. This book should be a requirement for anyone starting on their journey to become a Physician Assistant if they plan to succeed on interview day. By reading this book in its entirety you are directly influencing the likelihood of your success during one of the most important interviews of your life.

I wish you nothing but the best on your journey and genuinely hope that this resource aids you in your pursuit to become a PA.

Brian Palm, PA-C
Founder of myPAresource and PA School Prep

HELLO FUTURE PA!

I'm so excited to help you on this journey. After finally submitting your applications for physician assistant (PA) school, the next step is preparing for interviews that will (hopefully) follow. The personal statement is the most important part of your written application, but the interview will gain you admittance and secure your spot in the program. Obviously you want to nail it, walk out of the room confident you did your best, and expect a congratulatory call or letter sooner rather than later.

In this book, you'll learn how to think beyond the questions, and develop strong, thoughtful, mature answers. This guide is for PA school candidates determined to shine in their interviews, and willing to put in the work to become a PA. It is not my goal to give you verbatim answers to memorize and regurgitate. I want you to dig deep and spend time thinking about what the following questions mean to you personally.

As someone who has recently gone through the process of applying to PA school, and gained multiple acceptances on my first attempt, I understand where you're coming from as an applicant, but also the perspective of what the PA programs are looking for.

Working with hundreds of students through mock interviews, and instilling the confidence and knowledge essential to leaving a good impression, it is gratifying to know many have achieved acceptance. Because I assisted with admissions while in PA school, I can provide insight to make your answers stand out. I know what your interviewers are looking for.

By reading this book and completing the exercises, you will understand common questions asked during PA school interviews. I will guide you in what to include in your answers, as well as what to avoid. I will teach you to not just answer the question, but show maturity and provide the information your interviewer actually wants to know. While I don't guarantee every single question you could possibly encounter is within this book, there are over 300 questions, and when you're done, you will be able to confidently identify why a question is being asked instead of focusing on wording.

I promise if you read this book, and learn how to think about questions differently, you will feel confident at your next PA school interview. You will show the admissions panel who you are as a person, what you will bring to their class, and the type of PA you aspire to be in the future.

So, it's time to start preparing! Whether or not you've received an initial invitation to interview or you are preparing for your 20th interview, you need this information. Don't let lack of preparation stand in your way of achieving your dreams to become a PA!

I have curated the following information over the years I prepared for PA school and through helping Pre-PA students. So get to reading, and learn how to take control of your interview!

- Savanna Perry, PA-C
(*Your Personal PA Coach!*)

INTRODUCTION

Welcome to the book that is going to help you shine in your interview for PA school! My journey to become a PA began a few years ago and I now work full-time in dermatology while running a website called The PA Platform (www.thePAplatform.com) to help aspiring students reach their goals by sharing valuable information I learned along the way. When I made the decision to become a PA, there wasn't a reliable source of information to answer my many questions. I'm working on fixing that by offering weekly blog posts, monthly newsletters, and webinars. Another helpful resource is my podcast, "The Pre-PA Club," which can be found on iTunes or at www.thepaplatform.com/podcast.

I first learned about the PA profession during high school. My dad visited his primary care doctor, but saw a PA. Knowing my interest in the medical field, he mentioned it as an option I should consider. As a junior in high school, I was not too concerned with my future, but when senior year rolled around I began to think more seriously about my next steps. This was in 2008, and the information on the internet about specific requirements and different programs was lacking.

I attended the University of Georgia, and declared Biology as my major. This decision left my options open, and I still wasn't decided on the career I wanted to pursue. The idea of becoming a PA was in the back of my mind, but I wasn't sold yet. During freshman year, I researched and considered all types of medical and science based careers, including biomedical researcher, physician (MD or DO), high school teacher, nurse, physical therapist, dentist, and who knows what else. I spent way too much time stressing over that decision, and even shed some tears, but by the end of freshman year I decided PA was the best option.

I started shadowing, took a class for my certified nursing assistant (CNA) license and struggled through organic chemistry, while wondering if all this work was going to be worth it. The prerequisite classes required for PA school are no joke. I was taking the same classes as my pre-med friends, plus additional courses they did not even need for medical school. As you will learn, I'm a very detail-oriented person and spent hours researching the limited resources for what it takes to catch the eye of PA programs. I felt prepared when it came time to apply, but still terrified. My family and friends said, "Don't worry, you'll definitely get in!" but that's not too comforting when you know thousands of other people have worked just as hard for the same spot.

To obtain my patient care experience hours, I spent a summer working full-time as a CNA in a rehabilitation hospital. It was a humbling experience, and not a position I wanted forever. I have a ton of respect for CNAs. That job showed me the importance of teamwork in healthcare, and why every person on a healthcare team is important.

The summer before my senior year of college, I applied to the four PA programs in Georgia as soon as possible, even though I clearly didn't meet the requirements for two of the programs. I ended up with interviews at the two programs I qualified for, the Medical

College of Georgia (now Augusta University) and South University. I was automatically rejected for not having enough healthcare hours by the other two programs. It was expected, but still kind of stung. I prepared for interviews by scouring the internet for information, reading the one book that was available, and doing a mock interview with a PA I shadowed (which was the most helpful thing in my opinion).

My first interview was at MCG, and I was in the first interview group of the season. My suit was ready, and I tried to maintain composure. It was my top choice because it's a public program with lower tuition cost. My pre-med boyfriend was applying to medical school at the time and we had our fingers crossed for two acceptances from MCG.

The interview seemed to go okay from what I could tell. Even though I was shaking throughout the 15 minute one-on-one interview (which felt like it took forever), I tried to appear confident. Fake it 'til you make it, right? My interviewer was known for being tough, but previous students warned if I could impress her, it would benefit me greatly. I left the interview hoping I said something right and made an impression with my interviewers!

While waiting to hear from MCG, I was offered an interview at South University. I felt much less nervous this time, and I was able to be more comfortable. Fifteen minutes after leaving the South campus, I got a call from MCG with the exciting news that I was accepted. It was an amazing feeling, and one I hope you'll experience soon.

I graduated from UGA a semester early to give myself a few months to prepare and relax before starting PA school (which I would definitely recommend if possible), and started PA school in May of 2012. The program was tough, but totally worth it. While in school, I was asked to assist with interviews occasionally and I loved interacting with the potential new students. By having an inside look at the admissions process, I learned a lot about what to do, and more importantly, what NOT to do.

I'm thankful for all of my experiences, and I've made it my mission to help others achieve their goals. With healthcare changing so rapidly, there's a need for providers, and PA school is getting more competitive every year. With my interview tips and advice, I intend to help you get the same acceptance call!

THE PURPOSE OF THIS BOOK

So what should you expect to get out of this book? When working with patients, I try to ensure they have the right expectations of the treatments I'm prescribing, so I'll do the same here.

I want you to know what to expect when you walk into your PA school interview, and while there is always the possibility of a surprise, the more work, research, and practice you put in, the better you'll be prepared. There's no way I can take away all of your nerves, but I hope to at least calm them by instilling confidence and developing your interview skills. I also want to help you prepare for different types of questions, and focus on what the admissions committee is looking for instead of getting hung up on the wording of questions. Throughout this book, I've provided over 300 examples of questions typically asked in PA school interviews. Keep in mind there is no way to exhaust the list of ways questions may be presented or rephrased. The complete list of the questions addressed and the rephrased examples can be found in Chapter 15.

At the end of this book, you should know how to analyze questions and provide mature, thoughtful answers that stand out to your interviewers. We're not talking anything generic or boring here. I want you to have a reservoir of personal stories to pull from to make your answers unique and memorable. Your goal at this interview is to show who you are as a person, and how that will make you a better classmate and future colleague as a PA.

HOW TO USE THIS BOOK

If time allows, the best way to utilize this book is to read it from cover to cover, maybe even twice! The book is broken down into general information about interview styles and how to prepare, followed by chapters on question types. At the end, you'll find worksheets to help organize your thoughts and conduct a mock interview, as well as a master list of all questions listed throughout the book.

If you're in a time crunch, choose the areas most relevant to your upcoming interview. If you have some idea of the style and components, start with those chapters. Skim Chapter 1 for the type of interview, read all of Chapter 2 and Chapter 3, and then choose the Question chapter most relevant to your interview style. I strongly recommend reading Chapter 4 because these are the most commonly asked questions. Fill out the preparation worksheets in Chapter 13 to organize your thoughts.

Specific questions are presented in each chapter addressing various interviews styles of interviews. These questions demonstrate common themes and question types frequently asked at PA school interviews based on personal experience, discussions with faculty and students, and many hours of research. You'll find examples of how I would respond (which I don't expect you to memorize verbatim), examples of what NOT to say (very important), and how questions could be rephrased, while still addressing the same points. As I've stated, I want you to focus on WHY you are asked a question instead of how a particular question is worded. Just because a question is in the MMI chapter doesn't mean it won't be asked in a "traditional" interview, and vice versa. All types of questions are fair game.

Many people like to write out answers, but this isn't a technique I am fond of. Be careful not to memorize your answers and sound like a robot. I am a notetaker so I understand the appeal of writing. If this is the route you take, my recommendation is to use bullet points of quick thoughts and words that come to mind when practicing to pull from during interviews.

PART 1

GETTING READY

CHAPTER 1

TYPES OF INTERVIEWS

WHAT TO EXPECT ON INTERVIEW DAY

Have you ever been in a car wreck you saw coming? I was a passenger in this type of collision in high school. Even though we were stopped, I saw that the car turning left was about to get hit, and would likely collide into us. That split second was so strange because it felt like it happened in the blink of an eye, but time slowed down enough that I anticipated the impact and had time to brace for the crash. That's how interviews feel.

Each program varies in how they conduct interviews, and programs like to change up their methods occasionally. Imagine the difficulty of having 10-20 minutes of face time to choose a limited number of students to not only succeed in the program, but get along as a class. I'll present some aspects you can expect and prepare for, but be ready for the unexpected as well. Schools are looking for applicants who can be flexible and adapt easily without getting flustered.

For the most part, interviews consist of the same components: a tour, an orientation to introduce you to the program, time to interact with current students and meet faculty, and some type of face-to-face interview. Optional components may include an essay or group session, or even a quiz! Programs could let you know beforehand about a test, or just surprise you after arrival. Again, be prepared for anything. Go into the interview expecting the unknown, so you're less likely to be thrown off when something comes up you didn't prepare for.

ONE-ON-ONE INTERVIEWS

This is the most traditional type of interview. Programs may have you sit down with one faculty member, student, or PA as they ask questions about yourself and your goal of becoming a PA. This is nerve-wracking because it feels like you only have one shot to impress, but think of it as a conversation. Typically, these sessions are not very long, and may only last 10-20 minutes. That's a short amount of time to acquaint yourself with a stranger enough to tell them everything about yourself. Focus on what you think is important for them to know before you leave the room. As this may be your only chance, don't be afraid to open up and get personal.

In this situation, and any interview setting, there is the possibility that the interviewer has not reviewed your application thoroughly, if they looked at it at all. That is called a "blind interview," and is done to get to know you without stipulations of grades or the GRE. At this point, your application has been reviewed and you have put in the work to show you are capable academically. They just want to know more about you. You may have two or three separate one-on-ones during a single interview session. Don't be afraid to bring up something you already discussed in your personal statement or on your application because you can't count on your interviewer knowing about it. Additionally, the interview is an opportunity to add details you weren't able to include on your application.

TWO-ON-ONE INTERVIEWS

While similar to a one-on-one interview, occasionally two interviewers will ask you questions. This is a chance for them to use the "good cop, bad cop" technique, which means one interviewer is more intense in their questioning, while the other is supportive and encouraging. During any interview, expect the interviewer to build off of your answers and ask follow-up questions, which occurs more frequently with two interviewers.

PANEL INTERVIEW

If two interviewers weren't bad enough, sometimes a whole panel will ask you questions. I've heard of instances when the panel has up to 5 interviewers. Talk about intimidating, right? Instead of going into this feeling ganged up on, try to have a positive attitude. With multiple interviewers, you have more chances to connect and persuade them to like you enough to keep you around. Make eye contact with everyone on the panel and address them equally. It's awkward if you focus on just one interviewer or only speak to the table.

BEHAVIORAL/SITUATIONAL INTERVIEWS

The set up of a "behavioral" interview can take any of the formats previously discussed as this label focuses more on the types of questions asked. These tend to be more scenario based or ethical to see what your behavior would be in a particular situation. The goal is to illicit more detailed stories and examples for your answers instead of generic answers. Think "show," not tell. Chapter 5 goes into detail about how to identify and answer these types of questions.

MULTIPLE MINI INTERVIEWS (MMI)

Multiple Mini Interviews (MMI) are an interesting type of interview used often for medical schools. PA programs have started implementing this interview technique more recently. In a traditional MMI, you have 7-10 short, timed, highly structured interview scenarios lasting 5-10 minutes each. Think of it like stations. You will typically receive a prompt or scenario with 1-2 minutes to prepare before facing the interviewer for 5-7 minutes with your response. Fair warning, the types of questions in MMI can be just plain weird, which you'll see in Chapter 7.

The problem with MMIs is that each school does this process differently, and some are not what I would call a "true" MMI. Some have you move between stations, but they ask traditional questions. In a standard MMI, the interviewer will not respond to anything you're saying, either verbally or with facial cues. They may not answer questions and don't expect small talk. The prompts range from routine interview questions or completely random questions to ethical situations, critical thinking scenarios, or acting stations with standardized patients. This format assesses various qualities, such as decision making and communication skills.

GROUP INTERVIEWS

Group sessions can be presented in different ways, either an actual interview with multiple applicants answering the same questions or a group activity. Chapter 8 discusses these in more detail.

ESSAY

At times, a writing sample is part of the interview day. You receive a prompt to write about, and usually it's only a page or so. Programs will occasionally send an article to read before the interview, and then ask you to write in response to the information in the article.

The point of asking you to do a writing sample is to demonstrate that you can form an opinion and articulate it. This gives the admissions committee a chance to see that you are competent and confirm the authenticity of your own personal statement. See Chapter 9 for more on the essay component.

QUIZZES

While rare, a few programs include some type of test in their interview day. This may be a quiz on basic knowledge, like medical terminology or anatomy, questions about laws regarding PAs, general understanding of the PA profession, or GRE type questions.

Just know that if you've been invited for an interview, the program is confident in your capability of completing PA school. Unless told otherwise, this quiz is just to gauge where you're at academically or on subjects essential to doing well. Do your best, but don't freeze up and let your nerves keep you from completing the quiz.

EXPECT THE UNEXPECTED.

The golden rule. Occasionally, programs may throw something crazy at you. Whether it's an actual evaluation, or an attempt to throw you off with a crazy question, it's difficult to prepare for the unexpected. The better you are at being flexible and confident, the better you'll do in the interview.

An activity at one of my interviews involved pulling a question out of a fish bowl in front of other applicants and faculty to answer on the spot. It felt like a Miss America pageant, and there was a ton of pressure. Some of the questions were serious and others were silly, but this is one example of something out of the box a program might throw at you.

CHAPTER 2

BEFORE THE INVITE

Once your application is complete, the waiting for your interview invites begin! It's difficult waiting on the call or e-mail that could potentially impact your future, but while waiting, you can prepare.

INTERVIEW ATTIRE

A SUIT! For PA school interviews, I'm a firm believer in wearing a suit, whether male or female. Going to a job interview after school may be more laid back and business casual would be acceptable, but for this all-important interview I recommend a suit. It's better to be overdressed than underdressed in this particular scenario. While it may sound a little sexist, I was given the advice for my interview that females should wear a pantsuit (as opposed to a skirt) because it is one less thing that differentiates you from males. I don't know if there is truth in that, but I wore a pantsuit and all of the females accepted from my interview group were wearing pants. Probably superstition, but the thought is that it makes the interviewer judge you less on appearance. If you do wear a skirt, pantyhose are non-negotiable.

A suit doesn't have to be boring. Most people think all suits are black and that's not true today. I chose a light gray suit from Banana Republic Factory store, with a dark purple lace shirt underneath. Your outfit should fit well and look professional. For girls, you can show personality with a little color or jewelry choices. And guys, pick a nice tie with a pattern or some color if that's your style. As a rule of thumb, if you have to ask if part of your attire is appropriate for an interview, it probably isn't.

The director of one program gave me a tip before I applied. She told me they look for "mature" candidates at interviews. There's such a wide range of ages applying to PA school, and if you're a twenty-one year old who looks like a sixteen year old (like me), you want to fit in with the older interviewees. I wore three inch Clarks heels that were comfortable for walking around campus on the tour, and pulled my hair into a ponytail to make me look older, as well as get it out of my face and help me not to fidget.

Once you've submitted your applications, if you do not already own an appropriate outfit, start shopping. Should you get a last minute interview invite, you want to be prepared. You don't need the extra stress of scrambling to find a suit. Practice your hair and makeup ahead of time (yep, guys too), and get a haircut if needed. Well-groomed and professional are the goals.

DO YOUR RESEARCH.

You have likely spent a good amount of time researching the schools you applied to, but dig deeper in preparation of your interview. Find out what is unique about each school and what questions you have. Write this stuff down and study it before the interviews. Each program's website is a great resource, but you may not always find the information you're looking for.

Find the mission statement and review it to make sure you can address why you fit in with the program's goals. Also, read about the faculty. See if you have anything interesting in common, like an alma mater or hometown. Don't worry about memorizing everything, but these facts may come in handy for small talk and establishing connections to make you more memorable as an applicant.

A website I used while applying to school, and one I still find extremely helpful, is www.physicianassistantforum.com. This is the most active forum of Pre-PA, PA-S, and practicing PAs on the internet. They have specific threads for each program where people post their application status and often the interview layout and tips. Current students may offer advice and give a picture of what daily life looks like at a particular program. Applicants start posting when they get accepted, so you can have an idea of the timeline and hopefully find some of your classmates when you are also accepted!

There are a few resources available with the basics of each program, but some of these are not updated regularly, so make sure you're getting current information. On The PA Platform (www.thepaplatform.com), there are "Program Spotlights" with research on programs to give you current information, but refer to each program's website as well.

If you have a specific question about a program, and you aren't able to find the answer, it's not a bad idea to give the school a call. You don't want to be pesky, but usually the admissions department welcomes questions. You may even be able to locate alumni on LinkedIn or Facebook and reach out to see if they are willing to share their insights. There are a number of PA students and PAs active on social media, and if you find someone at a school you're interested in, feel free to reach out.

FIGURE OUT WHAT THEY NEED TO KNOW ABOUT YOU.

This is my favorite tip, and the one thing I believe benefitted me the most. A pre-health interview coach at UGA told me to sit down for 30 minutes to make a list of everything I wanted my interviewer to know about me before I left the room. This helped to ensure those topics would be my focus. When I was asked questions, I associated my answers to these topics and incorporated my examples. I like to call this "story manipulation," and I'll teach you how to do it in Part II.

This was great for me. Often in high pressure situations, like a PA school interview, our thoughts fly out the window and it's easy to be overcome with nerves! What you don't want is to ramble, lose your focus, and not get your point across.

By preparing ahead of time and identifying your pivotal moments, it's easier to stay focused. This includes specific personal experiences, struggles, or particular qualities about your character that are essential to who you are. Basically, what stands out when you think about your experiences? How have those examples contributed to your goals of becoming a PA?

The goal is to show the interviewers who you are as a person (not just an application), and convince them you will be a valuable classmate and future colleague. Being personal has been proven to make a huge difference, so this is a point I reinforce during all of my mock interview sessions. During an interview, utilize every opportunity to incorporate a story with a personal experience. This strategy makes you more memorable, and gives you a better chance to relate to the interviewer. These experiences can include anything from undergraduate, volunteering, shadowing, working, or specific patients.

One of my favorite stories from mock interviews is a girl I worked with last cycle who received plenty of interviews, but was struggling to gain acceptance. She came to The PA Platform after completing 6 interviews, which resulted in 4 rejections and 2 waitlists. She had one last interview scheduled. No pressure, right? As we started the mock interview process, I realized her answers weren't telling me anything about her. They were generic and impersonal, and while she was very sweet, that's not enough. After I delved into her history and provided feedback, she opened up and began providing answers that showcased her personality. Two weeks after her actual interview, I was so excited to get a notification of her acceptance.

When I start working with people during mock interviews, I imagine them as being inside an egg. (Stay with me here.) Every question is like a hammer working on the exterior of that protective shell to break it down and get to who you are as an individual. I wait to see how long it takes to feel like that egg has fully cracked and someone is actually getting personal.

Part of the difficulty with interviews is you are expected to talk about yourself, even brag on yourself. Many of us, myself included, are very uncomfortable with that, so you have to practice. If there's one time you need to get over it and talk about yourself, it's your PA school interview.

This exercise of thinking about what your interviewer needs to know and practicing talking about your accolades will help you take control of your interview once you get there. If you're only giving generic answers that anyone with access to Google could recite, you're not going far enough.

MOCK INTERVIEWS

Speaking of mock interviews, I recommend these because I think it helped me immensely. They say practice makes perfect, right? I met with a PA mentor occasionally, and she asked questions similar to ones she was asked during interviews for PA school. We were in a Chick-fil-a, so it was a little hard to concentrate with the background noise. Because of the distractions and my initial insecurities, I didn't answer many of those questions well. The practice helped me think about what I should say when asked again at my real interview. It also helps to settle nerves when answering a question you have already practiced. Although this is a service offered through The PA Platform, a good mentor or teacher may be able to help too. Chapter 14 is a Mock Interview Guide that will guide you to a more realistic experience.

Some undergraduate schools have a Career Services division that offers resources to help with interviews. The main concern is that your practice should be specifically focused on the questions typically asked during PA school interviews. If the service offered isn't familiar with the specifics for PA school interviews, proceed with caution, but additionally try to find a PA elsewhere. At The PA Platform, only practicing PAs with experience are utilized, making sure you get the feedback you need.

A mock interview should identify bad habits. Do you say "um" or "like" in between each sentence? Do you start every answer with "Ok, so" or another phrase? My signature phrase was "stuff like that," and I added it to almost every sentence. I would never have identified that quirk without practicing ahead of time.

Interviewing has an aspect of strategy involved. For example, figuring out what a question is actually trying to find out, and being likable more than answering questions correctly. For many questions, there is no "right" answer. Students get stuck on trying to use the right words or say the "correct" answer, and you lose yourself in the process. You want to answer appropriately and professionally, but in a way that makes your interviewer like you and establish a connection. You don't want to seem as if you've scripted your answers because they will sound dishonest.

It's fine to schedule a mock interview before hearing back from programs, but I recommend waiting until you are offered an interview so your session can be tailored to that school's style if possible.

GET UP TO DATE WITH CURRENT EVENTS

If you're not someone who follows the news closely, like me as a college student, do some research and familiarize yourself with current events in the nation and the world. Specifically, pay attention to anything that involves healthcare or affects PAs directly. Schools love to specifically ask about recent events, and it can throw you off if you aren't prepared.

The American Academy of Physician Assistants (AAPA) website (www.aapa.org) has great resources to shed light on what's happening in the world of PAs, particularly in their "Advocacy" and "News" sections. Don't forget about the power of Google either. I'll occasionally use the news feature to search "physician assistant" so I'm not missing any major events as they relate to PAs. The PA Platform frequently sends out updates and blog posts with important PA news to the email list. If you are interested in signing up, visit www.thepaplatform.com/email.

BE PREPARED TO GO!

Unfortunately, some programs do not give much notice for interviews. If you are taking a cancellation spot, you could hear just a few days in advance. While one to two month notice is nice, sometimes the call comes in on a Friday for an interview the following Monday. I've even heard of a program calling a local applicant the night before! With that being said, be on your toes! And check your spam folder often. A friend in my program missed her interview because it went to her spam folder, but fortunately they let her come at a later date. Turn on notifications for new emails on your phone or computer so you get those emails immediately.

Short notice can be tough with jobs and childcare, but let employers know of your impending need of time off for interviews. Have friends and family on standby for children or pets that need care. Most dates offered for interviews are non-negotiable, and you may not have multiple options of dates. If you can't make it, tough luck. That seems harsh, but there are so many qualified applicants and there is someone eager to take your place if you can't make it. Schools don't have the time or need to accommodate everyone.

PREPARE FINANCIALLY.

For PA school interviews, you are expected to pay for travel expenses, meals, and hotels. If you're lucky, breakfast or lunch might be provided. When applying to multiple programs and planning for multiple interviews, get your finances in order to cover these costs, which add up quickly. Put a little extra into savings or skip eating out during interview season if concerned about affording the expenses of interviews. It could be devastating to get an invite to a top notch program and be unable to attend because of finances. As a PA student, you will likely be supporting yourself on loans, so it's never too early to start saving and working on a frugal lifestyle.

Also, consider the fact that once accepted, a deposit is usually required within a few weeks of the notice to hold your spot. This can range from a few hundred dollars to a couple thousand. It makes no difference to schools if you are waiting to hear back from other programs. Be prepared to pay in order to hold your spot, and possibly forfeit that money, if another offer comes your way from a more desirable school.

AND THE MOST DIFFICULT ONE, BE PATIENT.

Waiting is so tough, and patience is a virtue. Right? It can be very tempting to contact programs multiple times to verify they received your application and inquire why you haven't received an interview invite yet, but this can backfire. While it's good to convey you are excited about their program, use a little self restraint.

Don't hesitate to call or e-mail should you have a legitimate question. Once everything is submitted and there's been no word (not even a confirmation) after a month, I'd call. And if they tell you to wait, then do it. On the other hand, if it's towards the end of interview season, you've been waiting patiently, and STILL haven't heard anything at all, I think it's fine to check on your status at that point.

One way to covertly check your status and let the program know you are still interested is to call or email with monthly updates. While it's great to update your application regularly in CASPA, the schools don't always look at it again. When you call, ask to speak with the admissions coordinator or program contact and inform them of any additional hours or courses you would like added to your file. (An email is fine too.)

CHAPTER 3

AFTER THE INVITE

Receiving the words, "You are invited for an interview" will be one of the most exciting moments of your life. With this great news, the nerves start setting in. You were selected because they liked what they saw in your application, and they want to see what else you have to offer. That should be a confidence booster! Try not to worry about the other candidates, and just consider the ways you would be a great fit for this particular program.

After you celebrate, it's go time. Make sure your suit is pressed and tailored, prepare possible questions for the program, and it's not a bad idea to scope out the area ahead of time so you're not lost on interview day. Whether flying or driving, allow enough time to get to your location and be well rested before your interview day. If a school has information sessions available, try to attend one if possible. Using the PA forums online (www.physicianassistantforum.com) can provide information regarding what to expect on interview day at your particular program.

TIPS FOR THE INTERVIEW

Now that we've gone over steps to take while waiting for the interview invitation, let's cover what you need to work on when walking into the actual interview.

BE CONFIDENT.

You got an interview! Awesome! Because of the strength of your application, a program would like to get to know you better, which should boost your confidence and provide encouragement as you continue preparations for the interview. The admissions committee already knows you want to go to PA school, and if they offered you an interview, they acknowledged you have excelled academically and extracurricularly and show potential as a future successful PA. Try to hold on to that confidence, and channel it for your upcoming interview.

Once you get to the point of interviewing, it's an even playing field. There will always be someone with a better GPA or more patient care hours, but that doesn't mean you can't bring something unique to the table. Help them put a face to your name and application during your interview. At this point in the game, PA school admissions are so competitive that experience alone is not enough to get you accepted. Show with confidence that you are the whole package.

IT'S OKAY TO BE NERVOUS.

You will be nervous. No amount of practice or interviews will completely erase those jitters. Your interviewers realize you are in a stressful situation that is very important to you, but the nerves can't get in the way of answering questions.

Take a deep breath, and if necessary, take a second to pause before answering a question. One strategy I coach on to help with nerves is to use the techniques you've learned from interacting with patients. You want to make a good impression and connect, so you'll smile and be a little overly friendly. Take that demeanor into your interview. You may feel like you're acting, but a smile portrays confidence better than a straight face.

KNOW WHAT YOU WANT TO TELL THEM BEFORE YOU LEAVE THE ROOM.

The interview is your chance to elaborate on information you've already provided in your application. It's normal to get nervous during your interview, start rambling, repeat yourself, and leave the room feeling like you didn't tell them anything about yourself. The Interview Preparation worksheets in Chapter 13 will help you pinpoint what has impacted your decision to be a PA and guide you in figuring out what information you need to focus on.

Here are some ways to think through this information with questions you should ask yourself:

- **How have you gotten to this point of pursuing the PA profession?** Really take time to think about this. It's more than just, "Why do you want to be a PA?" Think about when you first discovered what a PA was, and everything you've accomplished until this very moment. Think about the challenges you've been through in your personal and professional life. What have you learned about the profession through your research, shadowing, or healthcare experience? All of these things will be important during the course of your interview. At this point, you might feel slightly exhausted by the process of applying to PA school, so take time to rediscover your passion for becoming a PA.
- **What patients have impacted you?** These could

be patients who were difficult to work with, had interesting cases, or showed you something about healthcare. Every experience in the medical field should help confirm your decision and teach you more about what it will be like to continue furthering your career in this field. When I think back on my patient care experiences, I remember volunteering with hospice patients. I learned quickly that they would have good days and bad days and how to interact more effectively depending on their moods, which has helped me in dealing with similar patients as a PA.

- **What personal healthcare experiences have you had?** We are all patients at some point, and every encounter you have as a patient, or alongside a loved one, will influence how you will practice in the future. You will see good examples that you want to emulate, and bad examples you will try to avoid. Use these encounters to reflect on the type of provider you want to become and be prepared to articulate that.
- **As a PA, what are your goals for the future?** - Is there a field you feel strongly drawn to? Why? Think about what you want your role and impact to be as a PA in reference to patients, family members, your community, and also future PAs.

This process will be beneficial because it helps you recall what's important while in the nerve wracking interview. Obviously, you can't take this list into the interview with you, but you will have the thoughts at the forefront of your mind. You can't bank on being asked a specific question, therefore if you see an opportunity to interject information that's important to you, go for it. Don't hold back.

YOUR GOAL AT THE INTERVIEW - PORTRAY WHY YOU ARE A GOOD CHOICE AS A CLASSMATE AND FUTURE COLLEAGUE.

Let me explain further. PA school is fast. Within 2-3 years, you will be a PA just like the people interviewing you. This is why it's important to portray yourself as a professional, to instill trust and confidence that you will be a good provider. It's also important to be cognizant of what you can contribute to the class. PA classes are generally small and you see your classmates more than your own family. Everyone will have a better time if you make efforts to support one another.

PA school is unique in that it requires healthcare experience, and everyone's background looks different. Think about how your unique skills could benefit others. Can you draw blood and start IVs with your eyes shut? Are you bilingual? Do you have a unique cultural background that enables you to understand others better? Are you an older, more mature applicant who can share your perspective with younger candidates with less experience? Have you worked in a specific field for long enough that you'll feel comfortable helping others study that section? Are you awesome at making study guides and excited to share them with your classmates? Are you a parent willing to help the other parents get through the tough transitions together?

Even small things like these show your interviewer what their class could be missing if you're not a part of it. Instead of focusing on weaknesses and what you don't have, keep your outlook on your strengths. Each program tries to select applicants who will create a cohesive class of students capable of withstanding the mental and emotional stress the rigorous nature of PA school requires.

KNOW THAT THE INTERVIEWER MAY OR MAY NOT HAVE REVIEWED YOUR APPLICATION BEFORE YOUR INTERVIEW.

The majority of programs have interviewers that read over your information before the interview, at least to a degree, but occasionally you will have a "blind" interview. This means the interviewer has no information about you ahead of time. There are pros and cons to both scenarios. In a blind interview, you have the option to address anything controversial by bringing it up yourself. In an informed interview, you may be asked directly about a grade or discrepancy.

Also, you may be unaware whether it is a blind or informed interview, but the type of questions asked might give it away. If the questions are more personal, it's likely they've reviewed your application. MMI interviews typically are blinded interviews. Regardless of the type of interview, take time before your interview to look over your submitted information so you are well prepared for questions derived from your application.

USE STORIES AND SPECIFIC EXAMPLES.

Stories are more memorable than a general answer. If you can use a specific example to answer a question, it will make a better impression and help the interviewers make a connection to you. This is where your list of experiences and impactful patients will come in handy.

Many of these examples and stories can be used for multiple questions so having them in your arsenal will help you be more illustrative with your answers. This is what I call "manipulating stories" and there are additional opportunities to practice this in further chapters. The ability to pull different lessons out of the same stories to make them fit into certain questions is beneficial to ensuring you won't get thrown off by certain questions.

BE POSITIVE.

This seems like a given, but keep your answers positive. Avoid being negative or confrontational in the interview setting. If something difficult is discussed in your interview, use that opportunity to show how you've improved or are currently improving on the discrepancy. Take a negative and turn it into a positive. Also, remember that the whole day (or 2 days) is an interview, not just the time face to face with your interviewer. Even if you're told that anything discussed with current students won't impact the decision on whether to accept you, that's likely not true. You're observed from the moment you arrive, so be tactful in all interactions and questions.

Maintain this positivity when discussing other healthcare professionals. In an interview, never put down another profession. Even if you had a horrible experience with a physician or nurse, that doesn't inherently mean PAs are better or that we never make mistakes. You can discuss these situations, but be matter of fact about them, and not disparaging when describing the behavior of others. In medicine, there is a culture of supporting each other, even when a questionable situation might arise. This doesn't mean sitting back and allowing a patient to receive inappropriate care, but addressing issues professionally if needed and never directly to patients. The same goes for the interviews and you should show the ability to respect other healthcare providers even if you disagree with them.

ILLUSTRATE WHY YOU HAVE DECIDED TO BECOME A PA OR HOW YOU WILL BE A GOOD PA IN THE FUTURE IN YOUR ANSWERS.

It can be easy to get off topic in your interview, and a conversational interview is awesome, but don't forget why you're there. You must show them why you are the best candidate possible for a spot in their PA program. This is not to contradict where I said they already know you want to be a PA because this is different. I'm talking about providing additional details and specific examples to show the admissions committee specific aspects of your character that will make you a great provider in the future. Should you feel as if you're getting off topic, direct your answers back to the fact that you have dedicated a lot of thought into this process and you are ready to get the education you need to be a PA.

When I conduct mock interviews, I talk about this being "full circle." When using your story or example, explain what happened, address the lesson learned, and make a connection to how this principle will continue with you throughout your education as a PA student and into your career as a PA.

CONSIDER BRINGING UP ANYTHING QUESTIONABLE BEFORE YOU ARE ASKED ABOUT IT.

While evaluating your application, is there anything you dread being asked about? What makes you anxious when you look back on your information? This could be so many different things, such as low GPA, failed or withdrawn courses, lack of healthcare experience or shadowing hours, low GRE score, difficulty understanding English, etc. There's a reasonable chance if an area on your application is lacking, it could be addressed. Personally, I think it's better to take the initiative by bringing up anything negative to use it as an opportunity to show improvements you've made. This characterizes maturity and professionalism.

We'll discuss how to do this effectively in the next few chapters. Basically, you want to address any negative as a positive with a major focus on the lesson gained and how the experience will make you a better PA student and eventually PA.

BE HONEST.

This should be obvious, don't make stuff up. Beyond telling a flat out lie, avoid exaggerating the truth or discussing a topic you are not truly familiar with. If you aren't sure or don't have an answer, be honest. Don't dig a hole that could be difficult to get out of.

I see this most frequently when people start to discuss laws and legalities surrounding the PA profession. There's no denying this topic is difficult to understand, but don't pretend to have a handle on it when you actually have no idea what you're talking about. To give an example, a girl in one of my interview groups came out after her individual interview. She told us when she was asked about the future of the PA profession that she mentioned the Affordable Care Act. (**Bonus tip**- Don't discuss specific interview questions with people at your same interview! Especially if they haven't interviewed yet.) She was then asked, "What is the Affordable Care Act?" She had no idea. Big hole, and couldn't get out of it. She was not in my class the next year.

If you don't know the answer to the question, it's better to be humble and own up to it. Your interviewers don't necessarily expect you to be well versed in every single aspect surrounding the PA profession. You're interviewing to be a PA student, so those are the things they are going to teach you! It's worth practicing how to respond when you don't know the answer to a particular question. Here are some examples of responses:

- That's a great question. I haven't thought about that before. I'd like to do some research and learn more.
- Gosh, that's a tough one. Would you mind if we came back to it? (They may never come back to it.)
- That's an interesting question. Let me think about that one for a second. (It's ok to take a minute to think, and better than jumping in with something irrelevant or wrong.)

BE PREPARED FOR QUESTIONS TO BUILD OFF OF YOUR ANSWERS.

Interviews with multiple interviewers can take a "good cop, bad cop" direction. The good cop will pose a question, and the bad cop may challenge your answers. This likely will be in the form of asking another question related to your answer or trying to get you to change your answer. This is a primary reason why you need to be honest in your answers because you don't want to be perceived as wishy-washy. Only bring a topic up if you can back it up. For example, don't mention the difference in the medical model and the nursing model if you don't feel comfortable explaining further.

For the PA profession specifically, the manner in which you handle these situations is crucial. As a PA, you are expected to be part of a team, but you must also show you can practice autonomy and independent thinking. A PA admissions committee needs to be confident that as a practicing PA, you will not blindly follow directions of your supervising physician without forming your own opinions. At the end of the day, as a PA you are responsible for your own decisions. Don't give in to the pressure and change your answer. Stick to your guns and explain yourself thoroughly.

STOP TALKING WHEN YOU'RE DONE ANSWERING THE QUESTIONS.

When interviewees are nervous, it's much easier to ramble. Avoid repeating your answers multiple times as this wastes precious time you need to help the admissions committee get to know you. When you have sufficiently answered all parts of the question, and are satisfied with your answer, it's fine to stop talking.

This will feel awkward until you practice, but you'll get accustomed to it over time. Since it's an interview, the interviewer will just move on to a different question when you finish.

PRACTICE ANSWERS OUT LOUD.

Whether you have an official mock interview through a service like The PA Platform, work with a PA or someone else, you still need to practice articulating your answers. Be careful not to over practice to avoid sounding like a robot. I recommend practicing questions in multiple ways. Start by writing out bullet points of thoughts you would like to include, and let your thoughts flow so you can organize them. Then I suggest videoing yourself to see how you answer. I know we all hate to watch and hear ourselves, but use these questions to evaluate yourself:

- Are you actually answering the question?
- Are you saying what you want to say?
- Are you leaving anything out?
- Are you stopping when you finish answering?
- Are you rambling?
- Do you have any bad habits - "um," "like," touching hair or glasses, repeating phrases?

Video is important because you know yourself better than anyone else and the impression you're trying to make. You may watch your video back and feel like you are watching a different person or leaving out important information.

THE STOIC INTERVIEWER

A word of warning - there are some interviewers who pride themselves on being "tough." You may be faced with an intimidating interviewer who refuses to smile, laugh, or respond to anything you say. They have the best stone face, which tends to cause thoughts like, "I'm doing terrible! They hate me!"

Stop! If they have this demeanor with you, they are doing it to other applicants too. It's not just you, and it is not a reflection of how you're performing. Instead of getting flustered, realize you've got this interviewer figured out. Impress them, and you'll be in a good spot.

FOR THE REAPPLICANT

It can be discouraging to apply multiple times and sacrifice the time and money to go to interviews without gaining acceptance, but regretfully it happens. If you are getting interviews, it means your application is strong. However, if you went on interviews and only got waitlisted or rejected, chances are you need to work on your interview skills. (That's what you're doing now, right? Good job!)

If you haven't already, contact programs that rejected you and attempt to get feedback on ways to improve. They may refuse altogether or give generic advice, but any critiques will provide some direction for next time.

One tendency after multiple interviews is applicants appear a bit jaded or bored while responding. I observe this frequently in mock interviews. I get that you're tired and over it, but strive to maintain the excitement and eagerness you had for your very first interview.

TOP 10 MOST COMMON MISTAKES

1. Sounding like a robot
2. Trying to say the "right" thing
3. Unprofessional appearance or behavior
4. Sounding bored and not passionate (Smile!)
5. Not thinking before answering
6. Going off topic and not answering the prompt
7. Being negative
8. Not getting personal enough in answers
9. Losing focus of why a question is being asked
10. Being generic

PRE-INTERVIEW PEP TALK!

Alright, let's say this together out loud. You may feel silly, but you deserve a pep talk before you head into your interview. Save this for the day of your interview for that extra boost of confidence.

I've got this.

All of the hard work, time, and money I've devoted to this goal over the past few years is about to pay off.

I'm going to walk in that room with my head held high and gather every ounce of confidence I possess.

I'm going to leave it all on the table and show these people why I deserve this.

My nerves will not get the best of me.

I'm ready for PA school.

I'm ready to be a PA.

Now that we've gone over how to prepare, it's time to jump into questions to start practicing and developing your answers. In the next chapters, we'll break down types of questions addressed in the different styles of interviews. While this won't be an exhaustive list of every question that could ever be asked (because there is literally an infinite amount), there are a ton. Get ready.

PART 2

THE QUESTIONS

CHAPTER 4

TRADITIONAL QUESTIONS

The traditional interview is my favorite. This version tends to be the most laid back, but the easiest for you to take control. This allows you to incorporate the stories that characterize your personality. The questions tend to be open ended and when they don't particularize a certain direction, you get to take the lead.

Even with the knowledge you're walking into a behavioral or MMI style interview, be prepared to answer the most common traditional questions. As we discuss these questions in full detail, throughout your preparations and practice, don't forget the main objective: convincing your interviewer why you are the obvious choice for a spot in their program.

It is your primary goal to show confidence in your strengths and your readiness to succeed in their PA program. If you are unable to answer the following 5 questions, you'll have a difficult time convincing them you are fully prepared.

THE BIG 5

- Tell me about yourself.
- Why do you want to be a PA?
- Why do you want to attend this program?
- Are you aware of what a PA does?
- What have you done to prepare for PA school?

These are the most important questions because they get straight to the point. If you have inadequate time to practice, these questions should be your main focus. Even if not asked these particular questions verbatim, this information should be incorporated during your interview. Let's dissect each question further.

1. TELL ME A LITTLE BIT ABOUT YOURSELF.

This should be straightforward, but the admissions committee really just wants to know about you as a person! There are varying opinions in regards to how you should address this question, but here's my opinion. When conducting a mock interview, I generally start with a version of this question, and it's honestly somewhat a trick question. I'm looking for whether you talk about yourself personally and if I learn something about you that's not on your application, or if you jump into talking about why you want to be a PA.

I obviously know you want to go to PA school, so use this question as an icebreaker to tell the admissions committee about yourself outside of education and healthcare experience. This is a chance to make a connection with your interviewer, and present yourself as a well-rounded candidate.

Talk about your hobbies, family, passions, background, and anything else important to you. Chances are this information can likely tie into your desire to go to PA school, and then transition into what you are currently doing on a daily basis. PA school admissions have become so competitive that relying on your healthcare experience is not enough. That worked 10 years ago when an abundance of hours weren't required as frequently, but now everyone has experience.

By bringing up interesting aspects about your life, you are making yourself more memorable. If your answers are generic, cookie-cutter reiterations from your application, your interviewers won't remember you. Sometimes the connections you make can allow you to have a better interview experience. Maybe you mention that you have a poodle, and suppose your interviewer is a fellow poodle lover? Now you guys are best friends!

Besides not providing personal information, another mistake commonly made is not actually introducing yourself. If you shook hands and said your name initially, it's ok if you don't want to reiterate, but I believe the more they hear your name the better. Keep in mind there are hundreds of applicants being interviewed, and you want to be the one they remember.

My response: My name is Savanna Perry, and I'm from Georgia. I grew up in a smaller town, and went to the University of Georgia where I majored in Biology. While there, I was involved in a campus ministry, and I continue to be involved at my church. I'm married and my husband is in medical school. I enjoy cooking, even if I'm not the best at it, but I'm getting better. I love doing craft and DIY projects and reading for fun. I have a passion for mission trips, and I've been to Jamaica and Amsterdam to serve in different capacities. Recently, I've worked as a CNA in a rehabilitation hospital and spent time volunteering with hospice patients as I prepare for PA school.

Ways to Rephrase:

- What do you like to do for fun?

- Tell me about some of your hobbies.
- What is the last book you read?
- What is your life saying?
- Tell me what your typical day looks like.
- Introduce yourself.
- What makes you unique?
- Discuss a pastime you enjoy.

2. WHY DO YOU WANT TO BE A PA?

Everyone has personal reasons for wanting to be a PA. Think back to when you first discovered what a PA was, either from research or a personal experience, and figure out what appealed to you about the profession at that time. Possible answers include the benefits of PA school over other medical programs, including working as part of a team with a physician, quicker and less expensive schooling, and lateral mobility (switching specialties). These are positives you are probably aware of, but you need to clarify what specifically draws you to becoming a PA over other professions. What personal reasons do you have for making this decision? PAs generally spend more time with their patients, due to not having the extensive expectations or complicated cases a physician might have. While shadowing or working, think about the aspects of being a PA that appeal to you.

When I ask this question in mock interviews, I want to hear a story. I'm looking for you to take me on the journey of how you got here, and I want to know the pivotal moments that have played into your decision. You need to show you've put the time and effort into making sure being a PA is the right choice for you. During an interview, these are the questions you should be able to answer:

- What made you interested in medicine?
- How did you find out about the PA profession?
- What stood out to you about the profession?

- Why do you want to be a PA for the rest of your working career?
- Are you passionate about this profession?
- What have you done to prepare for PA school and your future career as a PA?

In addition to this question, you may be asked if you considered other medical fields. Logically, to decide on PA school, you had to at least consider medical school because the end result has many similarities. Becoming a nurse practitioner (NP) is a consideration for many students because the course is similar, with again, a comparable outcome. Be prepared to further discuss any occupation you bring up, whether medical school, nursing/NP school, physical therapy, dentistry, occupational therapy, research, or others. The interviewers may ask specific questions about these occupations and question why you ultimately decided on PA. If you have a parent who works in the medical field as an MD or NP, address why you didn't choose to follow in their footsteps and how they feel about your decision.

Always be honest, and back up your decision by discussing work and shadowing experience, and how that provides confirmation. Remember, anytime you can use specific, personal stories your answer will have more credibility and be more memorable.

A common answer, especially for females, is that being a PA provides flexibility to have a family. While not a terrible answer, and you should be honest, that isn't the best primary reason for becoming a PA. I know many PAs who have worked for 2-3 years, started a family, and stopped practicing. Programs want students who will have a substantial career and contribute to the PA profession longterm, so it may discourage them slightly if your goal of having a family makes it seem as if you will not be fully dedicated to your job. I believe your schedule is up to you, whether a PA or physician. The reason you want to be a PA should be a love of the daily grind that comes along with the profession.

What NOT to do - Do not tell your interviewer that you want to go to PA school because you were unable to get into medical school. This should be a no-brainer, as that is not the student they are looking for. If your primary ambition is becoming a physician, you will likely not be happy as a PA having to answer to a supervising physician, and the interviewer is aware of this.

Ways to Rephrase:

- Have you considered medical school?
- Did you ever want to be a physical therapist?
- Why don't you want to be a doctor?
- What influenced your decision to become a PA?
- Tell me about your motivations for becoming a PA.
- Why have you chosen to pursue the PA profession?
- How did you become interested in becoming a PA?
- What part of becoming a PA and practicing medicine as a PA are you looking forward to the most?

3. WHY DO YOU WANT TO ATTEND THIS PROGRAM?

This is your moment to sell yourself as a student, and show you have researched the program and recognize why you would fit in specifically at this program. Figure out what is unique about the program, and what makes it stand apart from other programs. Even though you ultimately want to become a PA, there needs to be a reason you selected the specific program you applied to (besides just meeting the requirements). Start by thoroughly reviewing the program's website for information. If you know students at a program, reach out to them and find out what they love (or don't love) about their education. During the interview, you can bring up anything specific you have heard first hand to verify you did your homework.

While researching programs, here are some things to consider:

geographic location, facilities, focus on a specialty, opportunity for international rotations, cadaver labs, class size, community involvement, location of clinical rotations, cost, faculty to student ratio, PANCE rate, attrition rate. Be prepared to discuss what you are looking for in a program and demonstrate how this particular school will meet those goals. Location should be included in your answer to give your interviewer confidence you will stay once accepted, especially if you'll have to move a substantial distance to attend school.

Think about the skills and knowledge you have gained through your healthcare experience, and ways your education has been unique. What makes you different from the person sitting next to you? How can you utilize your experiences to assist your classmates? For example, if you have extensive experience with phlebotomy and starting IVs, that will be extremely helpful when classmates are learning for the first time. As an ultrasound technician, you can teach other students about ultrasound and answer questions. A background in research can be helpful because often a Master's project or research paper is required in PA school, and many people have never participated in extensive research. Maybe you're bilingual and can teach your classmates a few phrases or help translate on an international rotation. Get creative! Discover your gifts and sell them.

Consider your cultural or religious background. PA schools are looking for diversity because as a PA you will see patients from a variety of backgrounds. Part of PA school is respecting others and treating everyone equally. If you have faced adversity, use your story to help classmates as they interact with patients and each other. If you have immigrant parents or grandparents and you've seen their struggles with the healthcare system, you can educate classmates on how to make the process easier for these patients.

Other considerations are practical things. Are you a great chef? Will you bring brownies on test day? Maybe you were an athlete in college and will encourage your classmates to stay active. I would have never visited the gym if it wasn't for two friends in my program who invited (and basically forced) me to go with them. Show, don't just tell, the type of student you will be. Help your interviewer picture you as part of their class. In PA school, you want to be a good classmate and support your fellow classmates. While it is extremely competitive to get into PA school, once there, it's all about teamwork. Medical school is known for being competitive due to the pressure of landing a residency, so not having to deal with that competitiveness among classmates is another advantage of PA school.

As you can see, this is a complex question and extremely important. You need to be able to marry the concepts of what a program offers with what you are bringing to the table.

My Response: There are multiple reasons why I am a good fit for Augusta University and why I applied here specifically. Location was a huge factor because I'll be close to home and close to my support system who will get me through PA school, and knowing the area will benefit my classmates from other places. Being from Georgia, the lower tuition and benefits of state funding are advantages. I'm really interested in the cadaver lab because it's a huge benefit if I end up working in a surgical field as a PA. My decision was confirmed after attending the Closer Look tour, speaking with students and hearing from the faculty how well prepared graduates are coming out of the program, as well as the many resources available. I am aware of how rigorous the program is and the expectations you have for the students, and I'm confident that my undergraduate education and study skills have prepared me to excel in the coursework during PA school. Working as a CNA has helped me to develop strong time management skills that will also allow me to stay on top of the tasks I'll face during PA school. I've spent time volunteering abroad, and I'm excited about the opportunity to participate in the student run clinic while in PA school here at Augusta University. These are the reasons Augusta University is my top choice.

Ways to Rephrase:

- What makes you unique?
- What makes you a good candidate for our program?
- What can you bring to the class?
- How would the class benefit as a whole from having you as a member?
- What makes you diverse?
- What would our class be missing if we didn't pick you?
- Why should we pick you?
- What sets you apart?
- What is appealing about the location of (program name)?
- What qualities or skills do you have that would make you a valuable student and classmate?
- Why did you decide to choose a program that's out of state?
- Why did you apply to a program that's close to/far away from your hometown?

4. ARE YOU AWARE OF WHAT A PA DOES?

If you're applying to PA school, this should be a simple question! Although specifics depend on the specialty, level of experience, and supervising physician, PAs care for patients in many of the same ways as doctors. PAs can see and evaluate patients, take histories, perform physical exams, diagnose, recommend treatment, order and interpret labs and imaging, educate patients, and prescribe medication. Some PAs do procedures, assist in surgery, or perform surgeries independently depending on training and what both the PA and supervising physician feel comfortable with, as well as state laws.

As much as I've said to avoid generic or cliche answers, one exception is the definition of a PA. You'll be explaining your career to patients, family, and friends so you need to feel equipped to adequately articulate what you do on a daily basis. Your interviewer expects you to have a strong understanding of the daily roles and responsibilities of a PA.

Hopefully, you have spent time shadowing to gain a first hand look at the role of a PA in practice. Shadowing should either cement your decision to pursue PA school or create doubts, while providing exposure to healthcare and patients, which is a good talking point during your interview. Looking back on shadowing experiences, note what the PA did on a daily basis and the interactions with both patients and supervising physicians. While you may have seen an interesting medical case, the purpose of shadowing is to observe the career. This question is an opportunity to incorporate a personal story to illustrate your point and answer the question with shadowing or work experiences. If a particular PA stands out, talk about that time and how it impacted your decision to pursue your education to become a PA.

To summarize and make this basic, here's a one sentence answer: PAs are advanced practice providers who evaluate patients, diagnose diseases, treat patients, and prescribe medications under the supervision of a physician.

Ways to Rephrase:

- Explain the role of a PA to a patient.
- Describe what a PA does.
- What have you observed while shadowing?
- What have you seen that has influenced your decision to become a PA?
- Do you fully understand the role of a PA?
- Pretend you are asked to speak to a group of high school students and explain the PA profession.
- What makes you an ideal applicant for PA school?
- What do you see as the future of PAs?
- How do you see the role of PAs changing in the future?

5. WHAT HAVE YOU DONE TO PREPARE FOR PA SCHOOL?

You were offered an interview, so the program is fully aware you have completed their requirements and put effort into this goal. Your preparations include healthcare and work experience, education, volunteering, and shadowing. Which specific experiences stand out that will make you an exceptional provider at the end of your training? This is an opportunity to expand on additional medical training or volunteering and explain its impact. Don't waste your chance by repeating what's on your application. In a relatively short time period, you will be considered a colleague by the person interviewing you, so portray yourself as someone they would want to work with and represent the profession.

Any personal illnesses or interactions you have had as a patient are relevant and will impact how you want to practice, so these are good talking points if you feel comfortable. Whenever you are a patient, you will likely leave the appointment thinking, "I like how they listened to me," or "When I practice, I would never be rude like that." The big things for me personally are being respectful of patient's time, and making personal connections with patients so they feel confident in the care I give.

Consider the academic side of things too. You need to show the program you are ready for the rigors of PA school academics. Your undergraduate coursework provides the time management and study skills you'll need to be successful at the graduate level.

Ways to Rephrase:

- How have you prepared to be a successful PA?
- What specific skills do you have that will benefit you or your classmates during PA school?
- What experience in your background will make you a good PA?

6. WHEN DID YOU DECIDE TO PURSUE PA SCHOOL?

Theoretically, this question should be covered while discussing why you want to be a PA, but in case you didn't address this information, reflect on this pivotal decision.

When choosing a career, you devote serious time and thought into that critical choice. Therefore, it's reasonable for your interviewer to inquire about your motives. If it's a somewhat new decision, that's acceptable, but clearly explain the transition in your thinking. It's also okay if you don't have an epic story of how you first met a PA in the ER while you were having some rare illness.

My personal example is much more boring than that! I found out about PAs because my dad happened to see one for a visit while I was in high school. He mentioned it might be a good option for me. From that conversation, I did my own research and spent time shadowing to confirm my decision, but no crazy event brought me to my career.

What Not To Do: Avoid making it appear like this is a split second decision without much thought. A last minute decision or switch from a different career path is acceptable, but convey confidence in your decision. Using PA school as a backup plan or an easier or quicker option is not an impression you want to leave.

Ways to Rephrase:

- How were you initially introduced to the PA profession?
- How did you discover the PA profession?
- When did you find out about the PA profession?
- What have you done to increase your chances of being accepted to a PA program?
- What experiences have you had that will influence how you practice as a PA?

7. WHAT IS YOUR BIGGEST WEAKNESS?

The point of this question is not just to discuss a weakness, but to show you can recognize flaws, and work on self improvement. When you think about obstacles holding you back from being the best person you can be, what comes to mind? What do you struggle with the most? Keep in mind this is not a trick question, and ultimately you want to show your strengths. Some of the typical options applicants discuss include: time management, overcommitment, not saying no, and perfectionism. Besides stating the stereotypical answers, what is specific to you?

To attack this question, first state your weakness to make sure it is clear which weakness you are discussing. You need to explain why you consider this trait a weakness, how it has limited you personally, and the steps you are taking to turn it from a weakness into a strength. For example, if shyness is your weakness, you get out of your comfort zone by taking on public speaking. Address how this weakness will affect you in PA school or as a PA, and make it clear that it will not hinder your performance.

Bonus Points: Use a specific story to demonstrate your weakness instead of just discussing it. This is the perfect place to insert an example, and show instead of tell.

Ways to Rephrase:

- What is your biggest personality flaw?
- What would your co-workers say is your greatest weakness?
- What is one thing your classmates dislike about you?
- If you are not accepted into this program, what do you think would be the reason?

8. WHAT IS YOUR BIGGEST STRENGTH?

What makes you the person you are today? Think about things people point out to you most often. What would your co-workers say if asked what your greatest strength is?

Most people don't like to brag on themselves, so it can be difficult to answer this question. The most important aspect of this question is the focus on how a quality will benefit you in PA school or as a PA. Here are some examples that may resonate:

- Time management skills - Have you worked full time while going to class?
- Optimism - Are you the person giving out compliments and trying to keep everyone else positive?
- Compassion or empathy - Do you have examples of when you've connected with patients and gone above the expectations of your position to show kindness?
- Teamwork - Have you participated in athletics or worked as part of a close team at work?
- Study skills - Do you go above and beyond when making study guides or forming study groups?

Don't just state your strength, but elaborate to bring it full circle with an explanation of how this particular trait can benefit the program you are hoping to attend.

Ways to Rephrase:

- What makes you stand out compared to other candidates?
- What is the best thing about your personality?
- What would your last employer say about you?
- Why should we choose you?

9. HAVE YOU APPLIED ELSEWHERE?

This question calls for honesty, but exactly how much you share is up to you. It is perfectly acceptable to keep it short and sweet with a "Yes, I have applied elsewhere" without elaborating on each program you applied to or interviewed with. Regardless, you need to be honest. Some admissions committees look negatively on applying to one program. It can come off as arrogant, and look as if you are "putting all your eggs in one basket," to quote an admissions director. Others may disagree, but it's up to you whether you disclose the details of your application status at other programs.

Bonus Points: This is a great opportunity to go for a positive angle and make it known why you want to attend their program by showing you have researched the program and the reasons you applied.

My response: Yes, I have applied elsewhere. Although I would love to attend this program, my ultimate goal is to become a physician assistant. I applied to this program specifically because of the outstanding reputation, and the location is close to my family where I will have a strong support system while in the program.

Ways to Rephrase:

- If you applied elsewhere, how did you choose those programs?
- What would make you choose another program over this one?
- Where else have you applied?
- Have you interviewed anywhere else?

10. WHO IS THE MOST IMPORTANT MEMBER ON A HEALTHCARE TEAM?

While it's been mentioned before, teamwork is important in health-care, even more importantly as a PA. You have to work cohesively with others. When asked, reflect on times you've already been involved with a healthcare team. Keep in mind there is no "right" answer.

Consider the various roles that may be included in a medical encounter: patient, patient's family, physician, PA, nurse, PT, nursing assistant, pharmacist, and the list could go on to include respiratory therapists, occupational therapists, administrative staff, EMTs, and many more.

Your answer may differ from mine, and that's ok. When I think about the most important member on a healthcare team, it's the patient every time. In my opinion, if the patient isn't the central focus, no one else matters. Maybe your first instinct is the physician or PA who provides care with educated decisions, or possibly the nurses who monitor small changes in a patient's vitals. No matter who you choose, focus on the teamwork aspect.

Ways to Rephrase:

- How does a PA fit into the healthcare team?
- What is a dependent practitioner, and how do you feel about practicing as one?
- If you had to be a member of the healthcare team other than a PA, what would you choose?
- Discuss the relationship between a PA and a nurse.

11. WHAT IS THE BIGGEST CHALLENGE FACING PAS?

Probably just getting into PA school, right? It is a big challenge to become a PA, but there are other obstacles as well.

Since the PA profession is fairly new, we have more obstacles and issues than other jobs. You may have personally observed conflicts while working or shadowing that made you realize the medical field can be just plain hard at times. Reflect on these experiences to find your conversation points and show you understand the limitations.

For the most part, the general public does not have a clear under-standing of the role of PAs, which can be frustrating. One challenge is educating patients on the responsibilities of PAs, and helping to instill trust in our ability to provide quality care to patients. In addi-tion, some physicians and medical providers do not comprehend how a PA functions, so there are opportunities to educate within the medical field as well.

Legislation is another challenge PAs face because of constant changes and variations between states. There are specific rules pertaining to prescribing abilities and how PAs can be utilized in practice. As a practicing PA, it's your job to familiarize yourself with these laws and help maintain the autonomy of PAs.

Ways to Rephrase:

- What will be most difficult for you as a practicing PA?
- How do you feel PAs are limited?
- What are difficulties PAs are facing?
- What are the negative aspects of being a PA?
- What are some of the most significant issues PAs currently face and will have to face in the future?
- If you could change one thing about the PA profession, what would you change?

12. WHAT DO YOU EXPECT A TYPICAL WEEK IN PA SCHOOL TO LOOK LIKE?

To break this question down simply, do you know what you're getting yourself into? PA school is referred to as "rigorous," but basically, it's just really hard. In my opinion, it's not necessarily the information that's difficult, but the amount of material covered during the relatively short time period while in PA school.

Schools ask this question to give you the opportunity to prove you are fully prepared. It's not uncommon for students to withdraw from PA school during the first few weeks because the transition proves too difficult, and they become overwhelmed. Schools prefer to fill that spot with a student who will finish the program.

The best strategy for developing a response is to discuss the schedule with current students or alumni of the program to gain insight. You can possibly accomplish this while at the interview considering students are usually available for questions at some point. If that's not an option, ask PAs while shadowing what their typical day looked like in school.

To give you insight into my schedule, a week during didactic year consisted of classes on Monday, Wednesday, and Friday from 8 AM to 5 PM with various lectures throughout the day. Tuesdays and Thursdays were for additional lectures, small groups, or clinic time and the hours varied, but were usually a half day. Most weeks consisted of at least one test, but sometimes as many as 3 (especially if you include clinical practicals, called OSCEs). Sounds fun, right?

Be confident in letting the interviewer know you want to be there and how committed you are despite a difficult schedule. These are the keys to a successful interview.

Ways to Rephrase:

- What do you expect of a typical day in PA school?

13. WHY DO YOU THINK YOU WOULD BE SUCCESSFUL IN PA SCHOOL?

If a program is going to accept a student, they obviously want that student to succeed. It gives the program strong statistics and attrition rates, which improves their reputation and likelihood of maintaining accreditation. It's your job to convince your audience that once accepted, you'll be successful throughout the program.

The requirements for PA school necessitate rigorous coursework and excellent time management skills in order to receive a coveted interview. You don't have to repeat your entire resume or transcript to your interviewer, but explain how you persevered in your coursework to manage the stress. Think about your most difficult semester, why it was hard, and ways you overcame it. Essential skills you'll need to demonstrate include time management, stress relief, conflict resolution, healthcare skills that will benefit the class, and anything else that may give a unique perspective.

Ways to Rephrase:

- Assure us you will do well in PA school and not drop out.
- What study skills do you have?
- How do you stay organized?
- Have you been able to speak with current students?
- How many hours a week do you plan on studying while in PA school?
- What kind of barriers, besides financial, do you see involved with being a PA student?
- What have you done, besides shadowing, to prepare for PA school?
- How has your background prepared you for the intense physical and mental rigor it takes to become a PA?

14. IN YOUR OPINION, WHAT WILL BE YOUR GREATEST CHALLENGE IN COMPLETING PA SCHOOL?

Your answer will vary based on personal experiences and where you are in life, and there are different ways to interpret this question. You can attack it from an academic angle or from a more personal perspective, like balancing family and school. Without a doubt, the coursework in PA school is tough, and I haven't met anyone who does not find it challenging at times, so be more specific. Is there a particular subject you struggled with during your undergraduate studies? If so, focus on that as a possible difficulty you may face during PA school, but emphasize how you succeeded despite that struggle.

Being far away from family and friends may be another challenge. If this comes up, keep it positive and discuss your support system. PA programs need assurance that your family, significant other, and friends are going to be supportive and understanding while you are in school. If you mentioned having a child or family in your personal statement, be prepared for it to come up during your interview, which brings up the subject of "illegal questions." Technically, no question is "illegal." Possibly unethical, but not illegal. The programs should not straight out ask you these personal questions about marriage or children, but they may ask for elaboration on information provided pertaining to these subjects. I still believe honesty is the best policy and instead of shying away from these questions, answer openly and in a positive way to increase the confidence the program has in your abilities. It appears shady to avoid talking about the people who are most important to you.

Ways to Rephrase:

- Reassure me you will not fail out of the program.
- Is there anything that you foresee preventing you from completing the program?

15. HOW DO YOU STUDY BEST?

To excel in PA school classes, it's imperative to develop good study habits. Showing confidence in your study skills will help the admissions committee feel assured you can translate those skills successfully in PA school. I'm a note-taking kind of girl, so I study best by combining information from lectures, textbooks, and notes into a cohesive study guide. My guides were extremely helpful in PA school, not only to me, but my classmates as well. Some people like flashcards and some study in groups and quiz each other. Whatever works for you, go with it, but have a strategy to discuss. Another strength in school is using available resources and finding new mechanisms to assist in your studies if needed.

Whenever you are asked about academics, consider addressing any questionable classes from your transcript. If you had lower grades, withdrawals, or repeated courses, utilize this opportunity to put a positive spin on those experiences before being questioned directly. By taking the initiative, you'll get to explain in detail how you improved from the experience. Go into detail about how exactly you were able to overcome this challenge, whether it was adjusting your study skills or learning how to manage your time and give up some commitments, then use those points to relate directly to being a PA student.

Ways to Rephrase:

- Tell me about a time you struggled academically.
- Do you study best individually or in a group?
- Do you work better as an individual or with a team?
- How would you describe your overall academic performance?
- What will be your hardest class if accepted?
- How are you academically prepared for PA school?

16. HOW DO YOU HANDLE BLOOD AND GORE?

It's inevitable that at some point in your training or profession as a PA, you will be exposed to blood. Many PA programs learn skills, such as injections and venipuncture, by practicing on classmates, and you can't expect someone to take a stick if you aren't willing to be a pin cushion yourself. I distinctly remember having IVs started in both arms since it took me six tries on three different classmates to successfully place an IV. Programs are looking for at least a willingness to gain exposure to the messier side of medicine. You may have medical experiences to draw from and discuss using personal stories, but if not, strive to convince your interviewers this is something you can handle.

If you are concerned about this being an issue, try to find shadowing opportunities to give you exposure. Options to consider could be with surgical or ER PAs. The first time I saw a biopsy while shadowing in dermatology, I almost ended up on the floor, and now I do them everyday. During my shadowing in orthopedics, I also had some "seeing stars" moments, and while I deal with blood all day long, broken bones still make me pass out. Sharing these types of scenarios is beneficial to conveying how you handle graphic situations.

Ways to Rephrase:

- Have you ever seen someone die?
- Do you have a weak stomach?

17. HOW WOULD HAVING A FAMILY/CHILDREN AFFECT YOUR PERFORMANCE IN PA SCHOOL?

If you mentioned anything about having children or a family in your personal statement, or if you bring it up in the interview setting, this is a valid question. If this is a big part of your life, you should be honest about it during your interview. They will most certainly be affected by you being in PA school, but they'll also be the ones supporting you through it.

Utilize this opportunity to discuss how important your family is, but also the importance of your goal of becoming a PA. Naturally, part of the reason to become a PA is the ability to support your family and provide for them. When addressing this topic, make sure you are showing full confidence in your abilities to balance home life and school life. If you've already worked full time or completed classes alongside taking care of a household, use those examples to show you are ready for this. Have a practical plan for how your family will function while your time is limited. Does that include other family members helping out, daycare, nannies, or a spouse? Detail your strategy for getting through school and how you can commit to school with 100% loyalty.

18. HOW WILL BEING A YOUNGER/OLDER APPLICANT AFFECT YOUR PERFORMANCE IN THE PROGRAM?

Even if not asked directly, it's something to think about because either way it could be a strength for you! As a younger applicant, you may feel more comfortable with modern technology, and your study habits may be fresher if you are straight out of undergrad. As an older applicant, you bring your maturity and life experience to help younger students. Overall, recognize how your current age and position in life will benefit you and your classmates while in school.

Ways to Rephrase:

- What advantages or disadvantages would you have as a younger/older applicant?
- Do you feel comfortable with technology?

19. TELL ME ABOUT YOUR SUPPORT SYSTEM.

PA school is hard. There's no way around that, and having people supporting and backing you up will help you succeed. PA programs realize this, and want assurance that if you encounter a rough patch during school, you'll have an encourager to call for support. Use this question as reinforcement that your family/friends/significant other fully support your goals and want to help you get there. The convenience of technology can make the distance much easier. Give your interviewers confidence in your commitment to their program and to becoming a PA.

This question is more crucial if you're interviewing at a program significantly far away from your support group. Admissions committees could view this as a red flag in regards to your stability. Bottom line: they need candidates who will stick with the program for the duration. Do your best to give them no reason to doubt you are in it for the long haul and can confidently handle being on your own.

Ways to Rephrase:

- Who is going to support you through school?
- Is your family supportive of your goal to become a PA?
- Who has encouraged you to become a PA?
- How would you get to school?
- Where would you live while in PA school?

20. HOW ARE YOUR TIME MANAGEMENT SKILLS?

This indirectly relates to handling stress, but to succeed in PA school you must manage your time well and find a good balance of school and daily life. It's common to have at least one test per week, if not more, in addition to assignments, small groups, or clinical time. And that's just didactic year! There's also the need eat, bathe, and take care of yourself. If you have a family, you'll need to attend to them as well. Before the interview, evaluate your time management skills and determine areas you may need to work on. Whether you use a planner or have a strict schedule, know what works for you. Try to think about specific times in your life when utilizing your time management skills have been crucial to getting everything done, which presents a great opportunity to incorporate another story.

Ways to Rephrase:

- Are you able to handle multiple assignments at once?
- Are you able to handle a busy schedule?
- Tell me about a time you've had to multitask.
- Did you work while getting your prerequisites?

21. WHAT WAS THE MOST CHALLENGING COURSE OF YOUR UNDERGRADUATE STUDIES, AND WHY?

I can admit that mine was definitely organic chemistry. Hands down. I just didn't get it, and after too much time and tears, I accepted my C+. I had such a hard time that I questioned if I could really make this PA school thing happen. Many prerequisites for PA school are difficult, and your "most challenging" will depend on your intellect, school, and life experiences.

Think about lessons learned from your challenging course that will make you perform better in PA school. Classes that push us encourage learning academically and personally. Here are some things to consider:

- Did you develop better study skills or time management skills?
- Did you have to reevaluate your academic plan?

- Were you going through a difficult time personally that distracted you from school?

22. WHAT HAS BEEN THE HIGHLIGHT OF YOUR UNDERGRADUATE YEARS?

Hopefully, something stands out from your undergraduate studies besides tough courses, even if it's just graduating! There are tons of experiences that only happen in the context of college. That being said, I understand everyone has unique undergraduate experiences and you may not have had the "traditional 4-year college experience."
Take the experiences you *did* have and highlight what made them special. My fondest memories include mission trips to Jamaica and Amsterdam and football games every Saturday. It can be hard to pick a favorite, but reminisce about good times so you can be prepared to elaborate if asked to do so.

Also, think about how those experiences may prove advantageous in PA school or how you plan to continue to enjoy those activities. Many passions are discovered during school, so expand on them as you transition to graduate school.

Ways to Rephrase:

- What extracurricular activity will benefit you most as a PA?
- What was your biggest accomplishment from undergrad?

23. CAN YOU EXPLAIN YOUR LOWER GRADE/LOW GRE/LACK OF SHADOWING OR HCE?

Be prepared for direct questions such as this. Admissions committees may point out any weakness or discrepancy on your application, and they will have no shame in asking you about it. Even if a course was

10 years ago, any C/D/F or withdrawal on your transcript is fair game.

It's completely normal to struggle academically at some point. You should be able to discuss these topics without getting defensive or making excuses. Here's your strategy:

- *Explain the situation.* For example, I took organic chemistry during a semester when I had a full load and other difficult science courses. I was also working part-time and had extracurricular commitments.
- *Discuss why this was difficult.* For example, I have always found chemistry difficult, but organic was completely different. From the beginning, I had trouble grasping the concepts fully and recognized this course would take additional attention.
- *Explain your actions to remedy this situation.* For example, I looked for resources to help me understand the material better. I went to office hours for tutoring, used online videos, practiced problems continuously, etc. I asked my professor for advice on how to study more effectively.
- *Discuss the outcome.* For example, even though I received a C in the course, I worked hard for that grade and learned how to multitask and recognize when I may need to step away from some commitments to make coursework a priority. I can utilize outside resources to get a better understanding of difficult material and I retook the course to demonstrate I am capable of mastering this coursework. I successfully received an A!
- *Show confidence this will not reflect your success in PA school.* For example, the challenges I faced during organic chemistry have prepared me for the rigors of a difficult PA program, and the study skills I learned during this course will help me excel in your program.

What not to do: Make excuses. If there was a time you struggled or screwed up, you need to own it and explain it fully. Never put blame on a teacher for a lower grade. It's fine to discuss personal struggles you may have been going through (illness, family issues, etc.), but don't use them to excuse why you did poorly. Avoid giving your interviewer reason to doubt your abilities to do well in their program.

Bonus Points: Approach these topics yourself! If you know something is looming on your application that may be questioned, don't wait to be directly asked.

Ways to Rephrase:

- Are there any discrepancies on your application you would like to discuss?
- There's one spot left and it's between you and another candidate. The other candidate has a higher GPA. Who should be chosen?

24. WHAT ARE YOU LOOKING FOR IN A PA PROGRAM?

Before interviewing, identify what a particular school has to offer so you can brag on them. If you know current students in the program, talk to them about available resources and how the program functions. A good starting point is a program's mission statement, which must be displayed on each program's website. It should provide valuable information about the values, expectations, and goals. Other unique aspects to investigate:

- Cadaver lab - Full dissection means hands-on dissection on a cadaver. Prosected cadavers are already dissected and split into different sections for observation. Some programs use models or computer programs for studying anatomy. You may have a preference for one of these options depending on your future career goals.
- International rotations - Options for getting experience abroad are becoming more popular and desired. If you have a strong desire to participate in medical missions in other countries, you may prefer a program that offers opportunities to test the waters during school.
- Freedom in choosing clinical locations - This differs between schools. Some programs assign locations without much choice, and others provide more options. You may be required to stay in-state or travel. There are a few programs well known for their variety of rotation sites across the country, which may be beneficial if you aren't sure where you want to end up. If you have family or local responsibilities, clinical location may take higher priority. (Note - You will never be required to set up or find your own clinical rotation sites. It's a requirement that PA schools provide these for you.)
- Clinical experience during didactic year- Didactic year is mostly classroom based, but some programs do a better job of incorporating clinical experiences into this year than others.
- Class size - With a small class you are likely to receive more personal attention from faculty as opposed to a larger class that has more resources available and more students for collaboration. Speak with current students for their perspective on whether they receive adequate personal attention.
- Ratio of faculty to students - Having a low faculty to student ratio can ensure your access to help and attention

if you struggle during PA school. Having a low ratio can make a larger class feel small.

Ways to Rephrase:

- Why do you want to go to this specific program?
- What does our program have to offer you?
- What do you have to offer our program?
- Why did you apply here?
- Why would you choose our program instead of another program?
- What do you find appealing about (program name)?
- Why did you choose our program over the others?

25. WHAT ARE YOUR PLANS IF NOT ACCEPTED TO A PA PROGRAM THIS YEAR?

You must have a solid answer to this question! If not, it appears as though you haven't put enough thought into this whole process or that you are overly confident of your pending acceptance. Having a well-developed plan shows maturity in what you are willing to do in order to reach your goals. Basically, think about the ways you could potentially make your application better for the next cycle if you were to need to reapply. Here a few ways to consider improving your application:

- Take additional classes to increase your GPA or replace any grade discrepancies.
- Retake the GRE to increase your score.
- Diversify your patient care experience with more hours or experience in a new setting.
- Get a certification or further your training with more advanced certifications.
- Find more volunteer hours, and not just in healthcare.

- Obtain more shadowing hours, particularly in different specialties or settings.

In the event you've already been accepted to a different PA program, it is up to you whether you divulge this information. If interviewing at a more preferred school, it may be in your favor to let them know you have a pending spot and wouldn't be reapplying the next cycle.

Ways to Rephrase:

- How do you plan on improving yourself if not accepted into PA school?
- What would you do if you were not selected for this program?

26. WHAT IS THE DIFFERENCE IN THE NURSING MODEL AND MEDICAL MODEL?

A common answer when asked about attending PA school versus NP school is a desire to be trained on the "medical model" instead of the "nursing model." Be prepared for a quiz on what that means, and honestly it is difficult to find a straightforward answer on this one. At the end of the day, both professions are involved in medicine, just the fundamental goals of training differ.

In the medical model, a provider's goal is to diagnose and treat. In a medical program, you learn based on disease, and determine patient care accordingly with the goal of patient improvement. The nursing model takes a holistic approach to the patient in order to meet their daily needs. Although nurses gain extensive knowledge about disease while practicing, the major decisions about patient care are made by the primary provider. NPs are trained on the nursing model primarily in nursing school, followed by additional learning on the medical model to further their responsibilities while in NP school.

Both models of learning are extremely important and essential to providing high quality care for patients, which should be a common goal. Some individuals will thrive more in nursing, while others may do better as a PA, or a physician. Before you interview, consider an answer to this question should it come up, however don't broach the subject unless you are prepared with facts. To hear an interview with a nurse practitioner, check out Episode 13 of The Pre-PA Club Podcast on iTunes.

Ways to Rephrase:

- Did you consider becoming a nurse practitioner (NP)?

27. WHAT QUALITIES MAKE A SUCCESSFUL PHYSICIAN ASSISTANT?

Pull from shadowing and work experiences to provide the interviewer with a great answer, and interject what you've personally observed to back up your opinions. You need to verify that you can identify skills that make a healthcare provider successful, and show whether you have the qualities you are describing. We've all had personal and professional experiences interacting with different providers, both good and bad. Those times you've been the patient should help shape the type of provider you want to be.

Some characteristics to consider thinking about for an effective PA could include: compassion, kindness, flexibility, efficiency, intelligence, professionalism, optimism, a team-based attitude, humbleness, confidence, etc. I'm sure you can identify more, but with any characteristic you describe, be prepared to back it up with a definition and personal example if asked. This strategy will be much more effective than just listing traits, especially if you clearly reinforce how you will demonstrate these characteristics in the future.

My response: From my time shadowing Megan, I saw firsthand what it takes to be a successful PA, both with patients and co-workers. She was constantly going above and beyond for her patients by making decisions that were financially conscious, even when it took more of her time. She patiently listened to her patient's concerns, sometimes ones that weren't related to why they were there that day. She was professional in every encounter, but aware of her limits. One patient needed medication for a rash, but had many allergies. After looking through her books, Megan confirmed her choice with her supervising physician. I hope to emulate these same characteristics in PA school, and as a PA, it is my goal to be a provider who is compassionate, patient, supportive, professional, and humble in every encounter.

Ways to Rephrase:

- How do you plan to practice as a PA?
- If you were interviewing a potential PA student, what would you look for?
- If you were chosen to hire a PA, what qualities should they have?
- Tell me about the last physician you worked for.

28. DESCRIBE YOUR VOLUNTEER EXPERIENCE.

Hopefully by the time you get to your PA school interview, you have volunteer experience. There is no room for exaggeration on your application because it is likely you will be asked for details. Take a few minutes before your interview to look over your resume or

CASPA application. Review the experiences you wrote about to refresh your memory so you can discuss those activities more vividly. This question presents the perfect opportunity to incorporate a story and show a unique aspect of your character. Can you answer these questions?:

- Why did you choose that particular volunteer opportunity?
- What did you learn from your activity?
- How will your experience help you to be a better classmate or a better PA?
- Did you have a leadership role?

Ways to Rephrase:

- What extracurricular activity will benefit you most as a PA?
- What extracurricular activity will help you be successful in PA school?
- Describe a leadership role you have held.
- Do you plan on continuing to volunteer while in PA school or as a PA?

29. IS THERE A SPECIFIC SPECIALTY OR IDEAL JOB YOU ENVISION FOR YOURSELF AS A PA?

There are varying opinions on how to answer this question. You may feel pressure to answer a certain way if the program has a particular focus (primary care, pediatrics, surgery, etc.), but I go back to my cardinal rule - be honest. While being up front, try to remain open minded. You may be dead set on working in the ER after PA school, but that desire may come from time spent working in an ER if it's the only thing you know. Commonly, students come in wanting to do one thing, but fall in love with a different field while on rotations.

Many programs put a huge focus on producing PAs who will enter the workforce in primary care. If this is where you see yourself, that's awesome, and definitely let your interviewer know. If you're unsure, it's ok to let them know that as well, as long as you elaborate on possibilities. Spend time reflecting on experiences you've had up to this point and how those might influence your future decisions. By having a strong response, it shows you've taken time to really consider the impact you'll have as a practicing PA.

When addressing your career goals for the future, think beyond just becoming a PA in order to show maturity. How do you plan on giving back to your community and the underserved populations with your medical knowledge? How can you give back to the PA profession after graduation? Maybe you have considered having students shadow or precepting PA students. Another consideration would be seeking involvement in your state PA society or AAPA to help with legislation and general knowledge surrounding the PA profession. Also, feel free to address any personal goals you have that demonstrate what will be important to you in your future as a PA. This could include marriage or a family, or even a trip you've always wanted to take.

Ways to Rephrase:

- Where do you see yourself in 5 years?
- Where do you see yourself in 10 years?
- Is there a particular field that appeals to you?
- What are your goals in medicine?
- How do you plan to contribute as a PA professional when finished with the program?
- Why do you want to do primary care (or other specialty)?
- Why do you want to help underserved populations?
- Where do you want to work?

30. HOW WILL POLITICS INFLUENCE PAS?

This is a loaded question, and one that you do not have to delve into your own political beliefs to answer. If you're in the middle of an election year, you have the advantage of the unknown. Every 4 years in the US, changes are made to the healthcare system, and historically no one is sure of how this may affect healthcare or PAs. Through current news and journals, stay up to date with news surrounding the healthcare system to some degree.

As to how politics specifically affects PAs, you are not expected to know all of the ins and outs because even as a provider it is difficult to follow at times. Overall, as long as no new limitations are placed on PAs, it is likely there will continue to be a huge need for providers, thus the demand for PAs will continue to grow.

In addition to general politics, there's the dreaded "insurance" questions. Try to have a basic understanding of how insurance is affected by what's going on in the world. Besides having basic definitions down, consider how these changes may affect PAs. In the following "Ways to Rephrase," if there is a term you don't understand, research it and familiarize yourself. For bonus points, try to ask PAs you know, work with, or shadow how they feel about these topics. I don't believe you need to be an expert on these issues, but shoot for a foundation you can build from as a PA student and PA. You shouldn't be expected to understand insurance fully at this point. Even as a practicing PA, I can't say I'm an expert!

Ways to Rephrase:

- How do you feel Trumpcare will affect PAs?
- How do you feel the new health bill will impact healthcare?
- Tell us about healthcare reform.

- Do you think healthcare reform will be positive or negative for PAs? Why?
- Do you think HMOs and PPOs are good or bad for the PA profession?
- What are the trends of healthcare in the United States?

31. WOULD YOU FEEL LIMITED BY ANY OF THE STATE OR NATIONAL REGULATIONS ON PAS?

You need to do your homework on current events in the PA world, as well as any limiting laws or regulations. Most of these come from the state level because national laws specific to PAs do not exist. This is not a subject interviewers expect you to be an expert on, but it's impressive if you're at least familiar, and it shouldn't take too much effort to do a little research. Here are helpful resources to find current information:

- AAPA.org - Advocacy and News sections
- Google - Look up the state you'll be interviewing in along with "physician assistant laws." Usually this takes you to the main medical board website, but it can be difficult to tease out what the regulations are even there.
- Physicianassistantforum.com - There are state specific discussions where current PAs discuss issues they face, and you can ask specific questions as well.

Ways to Rephrase:

- Tell me what you know about laws for PAs in this state.
- What law do you think limits PAs the most?
- Are there laws you feel limit the PA profession unfairly?
- Are there laws you feel should be passed to further the progression of the PA profession?

- If you could change any law pertaining to the PA profession, what would you change, and why?
- Are you familiar with any national or state level regulations for PAs?
- Are you aware of recent changes in legislation regarding what PAs can and cannot do?

32. WHAT ARE YOUR THOUGHTS ON THE NEWER ONLINE PA PROGRAMS?

We're getting into more controversial "PA current events" now. A few programs have tried starting remote online PA programs, and while it hasn't caught on yet, there are schools exploring this concept. It's likely these will continue popping up in the future, with Yale as the frontrunner of this initiative.

As with other controversial subjects, you have to weigh the pros and cons of each side, and ultimately pick the one you agree with most. Show you can have well-rounded views by presenting the opposing opinion, but ultimately you need a definitive opinion.

There are no right or wrong answers because they are strictly based on opinion. For this question, pros to having online PA programs would be a greater number of PAs graduating each year, the ability for people in remote locations to attend school without moving, and more flexibility for families. While those are the positives, consider the possible negatives too: would online PA programs decrease the effectiveness of hands-on classroom instruction, thus producing PAs who are not as prepared? Another concern is whether programs are being created too rapidly, which could potentially result in PAs who are unable to administer the quality care that PAs are respected for.

33. WHAT ARE YOUR THOUGHTS ON THE NEW BRIDGE PROGRAMS FROM PA TO MD/DO?

Definitely a controversial topic! It's assumed that if you want to become a PA, you've done enough research to recognize the differences between a PA and a physician and you're ok with those. This question helps schools tease out whether you actually understand what you're getting into, while inquiring to see if you have underlying desires to go to medical school.

There are a few programs proposing "bridge" programs that basically provide supplemental education, allow you to take the required tests for medical school, and then apply for residency. The time commitment ends up being the same as if you initially went to med school. Most PA schools don't support these programs because they want to produce PAs, not MDs. Tread carefully when answering this question!

Ways to Rephrase:

- Are you using PA school as a stepping stone to become an MD/DO?
- Should PA education be standardized?

34. WHAT ARE YOUR THOUGHTS ON THE NAME "PHYSICIAN ASSISTANT," AND THE PUSH TO CHANGE TO "PHYSICIAN ASSOCIATE?"

This is a fun topic that some PAs have strong opinions on! Some feel the word "assistant" is demeaning to the PA profession and makes patients less likely to trust the actions of a PA. AAPA's current position is that all physician assistants should introduce themselves as "PA," and avoid saying the word "assistant" or "associate" altogether. Some programs have jumped on the "physician associate" bandwagon, and changed the name of their program. You'll also see "associate" popping up on resumes or LinkedIn accounts of name change supporters. Whatever your opinion, you need to pick a side and be prepared to explain your choice. Also, you should know this is a current debate before walking into your interview.

Personally, I feel it's simply a name, and the bigger issue is patients misunderstanding what PAs are. I don't think changing part of the name will make patients more educated, and I think it will actually just cause confusion. Do you agree or disagree?

35. WHAT DO YOU KNOW ABOUT THE HISTORY OF THE PA PROFESSION.

If you're interested in a particular career path, knowing background on the profession is essential. Since the PA profession is fairly new, it has changed from a gateway for veterans to use medical skills they developed in the field to a way for patients to receive high quality care with shorter wait times. Don't feel pressured to memorize every detail about how the PA profession was created, but have a general idea of the motives that drove the formation. A quick internet search should provide most of the information you need, but here's a time-line from AAPA of highlights to answer this question:

- 1960s - There is a shortage of providers.
- 1965 - The very first PA class of four Navy Corpsmen is started at Duke University by Eugene Stead, MD.
- 1967 - The first PA class graduates from Duke.
- 1970s - The concept of PAs gains momentum and a standardized process for accreditation and certification is established.
- 2017 - Over 100,000 PAs celebrated the PA profession's 50th anniversary!

Source: https://www.aapa.org/about/history/

CHAPTER 5

BEHAVIORAL QUESTIONS

Behavioral or situational questions differ slightly from traditional, but are often addressing the same topics, just phrased differently. By changing the wording of a question, your interviewer elicits a more specific answer. Here's an example:

How do you handle stress?

vs

Tell me about a time you've been in a stressful situation.

Think about how differently you would answer these questions with the variations in wording. Usually if asked a direct question, like the first example, you will give a list of personal strategies to relieve stress, such as exercise, cooking, prayer, reading, etc! But if asked to discuss a specific time you were stressed, you will likely provide a story, such as a particularly tough day or an overwhelming semester.

When using specific stories and examples, there are a few points you want to emphasize so your story doesn't seem random or too lengthy. Here's what I recommend:

- *Briefly explain the scenario, and establish your role.* For example - I was working as a medical assistant, and we had 40 patients on the schedule that day. It was my responsibility to room patients, get their vitals, and take a history.
- *Acknowledge why this situation was relevant to the question.* For example - This was stressful because our patient load was usually 30, and the other medical assistant was out that day.
- *Discuss your response and the outcome of the scenario.* For example - I knew organization would be essential, so I checked the schedule regularly to stay on top of patient's arrival times. Periodically, I checked the patient charts when I had down time to prepare for the upcoming visits.
- *Explain what you gained from this situation.* For example - While it was a stressful day, I learned I am capable of multitasking and I improved my time management skills. For example, I had to return patient calls during breaks, and stay attentive to the schedule to be efficient with my time.
- **Bonus points -** *Relate your story to PA school or being a PA specifically.* For example - I realize in PA school I'll be extremely busy with multiple courses and assignments to juggle, and as a PA I will probably have busy days as well. The time management skills I've learned from these stressful situations as a medical assistant have prepared me to prioritize well so I can provide the highest quality of care to my future patients.

Behavioral interviews are also similar to MMI style because they are somewhat scenario based in an effort to evaluate your behavior in a particular situation. You will likely be asked traditional questions as well, but expect additional questions based on specific issues. The goal of these questions is to evaluate your problem solving skills and ethical decision making. Keep in mind, the patient's well-being is always your main priority.

1. WHAT IS THE MOST SELFLESS THING YOU HAVE EVER DONE?

This is one of the toughest questions I've heard at an interview because it is designed to catch you off guard. One issue I've witnessed during mock interviews is some people don't understand what "selfless" means. Basically, it's the opposite of "selfish." If you don't understand the meaning of a question during an interview, you have two choices. Try to answer regardless and take the risk of not actually addressing the question or ask for clarification, which is my recommendation.

Selfless - concerned more with the needs and wishes of others than with one's own; unselfish

---

Thanks Webster! This question is difficult because as humans, we tend to be selfish more often than selfless. I've found people respond to this question in two different ways. Some have an automatic response that comes to mind, and usually it's substantial, like taking in a foster child or giving up an amazing opportunity to take care of a sick family member. Everyone else just blanks.

While this isn't a commonly asked interview question, there is an important lesson. Your answers do NOT have to be dramatic, intense stories. That is where applicants struggle because without an amazing example, they feel their answer isn't sufficient, which is not true. This goes for anytime you are asked for an example. Simple is okay.

Here was my response, which you will likely find less than enthralling. On the way back from a college mission trip to Amsterdam, a team member was feeling airsick. Her seat was alone in the back of the plane and my seat was in the front with the rest of the team. I offered to switch seats and sit by myself in the back of the plane for the ten hour trip. Not a big deal right? At 21, this was the best example I could give on the spot. Not because I don't do good deeds, but many times small, selfless acts go unnoticed. Don't worry if your answer isn't extravagant, as long as it's honest and demonstrates understanding of the concept.

2. WHAT IS THE BIGGEST RESPONSIBILITY YOU HAVE EVER BEEN TASKED WITH?

This is another question that varies greatly based on your life experiences thus far. If you are a younger applicant, there's a strong possibility your responsibilities have been limited. In contrast, if you are a parent, you are responsible for another person's life! Roles look different for each individual, but this goes back to the concept from the previous question in regards to not having to share a particularly shocking example.

Responsibility plays a huge part of being a PA, due to the fact you are caring for someone else's health. Articulating the responsibilities you've held in the past will translate to confidence as a healthcare provider.

Another way to think about this topic is by subbing "leadership role" for "responsibility." If you've held a leadership position, you've also had responsibility. Get creative, even if the best thing you can think of is taking care of your pet guinea pig as a kid (well, maybe try to come up with something better than that).

3. DESCRIBE A TIME YOU HAD TO OVERCOME ADVERSITY.

The word "adversity" triggers anxiety, especially if you don't understand the meaning. As previously stated, if unsure of what the question is asking, don't hesitate to ask for clarification. Let's have

Webster define "adversity" so we can address this question correctly:

Adversity - a state or instance of serious or continued difficulty or misfortune

---

Basically, this question is asking you to address a challenge you've faced, but not necessarily a huge event. The actual challenge is not as significant as the steps you've taken to overcome this issue.

At 21 years old, I could not recollect many times of difficulty, so I thought of times I felt I had been unfairly judged. I've always looked younger than my age. At 21, I barely looked 15, and if I was lucky, maybe 16. Even now, I get carded at R-rated movies and patients constantly question my age. (Everyone says I'll love it when I'm older.)

During college while working in the hospital as a CNA, it was always assumed that I was a high school volunteer or visiting a family member and definitely not an actual employee. And certainly not a college student who went through the appropriate training! I found myself repeatedly explaining my role as a caregiver to patients and their families, and I could not get frustrated or offended by their doubts.

Bonus points for connecting your story back to being a PA, right? For my example it was simple to make the connection. As a PA, I not only have to explain my age, but also my job. Many patients still don't understand the role of a PA. The continuous explanations as a CNA have translated into my daily life as a PA. Like discussed at the beginning of the chapter, address the lesson you learned from any scenario, and make it relate to your future career.

Ways to Rephrase:

- What is the biggest challenge you've ever faced?
- Tell me about a time you've been judged unfairly.
- Discuss a time you were unable to meet someone's expectations.
- What is the most difficult thing you've ever done?

4. WHAT IS YOUR BIGGEST REGRET?

When you look back on your life, there are likely stand out situations you wish you could change. But why would you want to change them? That's what this question is getting at. Not only what is your regret, but why do you regret it?

While attempting to answer this question, there are various scenarios to consider. Past decisions or actions are going to be the easiest to think of, but also consider missed opportunities, such as something you said "no" to and wish you hadn't.

It feels like a loaded question, but it doesn't have to be anything major. Even something simple like taking an extra class one semester that resulted in struggle could be a regret. You can use this as an opportunity to discuss academic struggles if you haven't had the chance to address those yet.

Ways to Rephrase:

- What one thing would you change about your undergraduate experience?
- Why did you choose your undergraduate major? Are you happy with your choice?
- What is one thing you would like to change about yourself?

5. DESCRIBE A DISAPPOINTING MOMENT FROM YOUR LIFE.

You're going to notice a pattern with many of these questions because as in other examples, it's not really about the "disappointing moment," but how you reacted and what you took away.

One of the most frustrating things that occurs while conducting mock interviews is when a student tells me they've never had the type of experience I ask about. Everyone has had a disappointing moment, an academic struggle, or difficult patient. If you've had any interactions with the world, you must have had these experiences! Do your best to provide an example regardless of how insignificant it may seem to you. To say you've never had this experience is unacceptable.

Your interviewer specifically asks about a disappointment to learn how you react to unexpected outcomes and how you pick yourself back up. Disappointments could come from a variety of instances such as school, athletics, or attempting a new skill. Your disappointment could even be not getting into PA school the first round! What a great opportunity to discuss steps you've taken to improve your application for this cycle.

Bonus Points: Utilize this opportunity to address an unfortunate grade or particularly challenging semester because obviously those were disappointing moments. By bringing up grades instead of waiting to be asked, you can put a positive spin on the situation. Explain to the committee what went wrong and how you improved.

Ways to Rephrase:

- Tell me about a time you disappointed someone.
- Have you ever been disappointed?
- Tell me about a time you didn't meet expectations.
- What's your worst experience?

6. IF A STUDENT FAILS A TEST, IS IT THE STUDENT'S FAULT OR THE TEACHER'S FAULT?

Head's up! In an interview setting, it is never the teacher's fault! There aren't many interview questions with a right or wrong answer, but this is one of them, and if you say or imply a teacher is at fault, you will be wrong.

Now I know there are some terrible teachers out there and it would be extremely easy to blame them (one likely pops in your head right away), but that's not the route you want to take. At the graduate level, it's essential for you to have the skills to do well in coursework, regardless of teaching style. If you find your methods aren't producing the desired results, as the student you must readjust and figure out a new plan. When faced with a failure, you must take responsibility and look to improving instead of blaming.

Bonus Points: Discuss a course that was difficult because of a conflict in teaching and learning styles. You know by now it's always beneficial to use a specific, personal example. Don't make excuses, but discuss what you learned from taking that class and how you modified your own habits to succeed. This is a chance to discuss your study habits if you haven't already.

You can also reassure the interviewer that you are fully aware and comfortable with the many types of lecturers and teachers you will encounter during the quick-paced didactic year and while on rotations. Even if you did not feel empowered by a particular teacher, you can show maturity by being complementary. Further impress by discussing your past experiences to confirm your confidence.

7. TELL ME ABOUT A TIME YOU RECEIVED NEGATIVE FEEDBACK AND HOW YOU USED IT TO IMPROVE YOURSELF.

Whether coming from a friend, family member, coach, or teacher, it is likely you've received feedback to foster improvement. The purpose of this question is to ensure you have been faced with criticism, but more importantly to gauge your response.

As a student in any field, particularly a PA student, and ultimately as a PA, you will be criticized. Feedback is essential to helping you grow as a person and provider so it's not something you should view negatively. Not everyone knows how to give feedback in a kind way that encourages learning, but it's up to you to pull out the lessons to find improvement.

As a PA student, I failed my first pharmacology test. It was the first month of classes, which was distressing to me. I had 2 choices: become discouraged and keep my original study methods (which obviously didn't work out well) or humble myself enough to ask for help and fix my mistakes. After approaching my somewhat intimidating pharmacology professor and seeking guidance from my advisor, I remediated that exam and passed the rest of my pharmacology tests. I didn't love the process, but it made me a better student. Do you have a similar story from undergrad or your workplace?

Ways to Rephrase:

- Discuss a time that you received constructive criticism and how you responded.

8. DESCRIBE A TIME YOU HAVE STRUGGLED ACADEMICALLY, AND HOW YOU DEALT WITH IT.

Please don't say that you've never struggled academically. Even if you are a genius, there has to be an area that was slightly more difficult for you. Unless you have received perfect 100's for your entire life, you've had an academic challenge.

Programs inquire to discover how you handle pressure in a school setting. PA school is difficult and there will be challenging subjects which require coping mechanisms to overcome issues and still succeed.

For me, this was Organic Chemistry, particularly the second semester. I didn't have a great understanding from the first semester because I relied heavily on memorization. When it came time to apply the knowledge, I struggled. Accompanied by test anxiety and tears, I knew I had to persevere to achieve the best grade possible. After hours of studying and practice, extra tutoring sessions and office hours, I ended that semester with a C+. I'm not proud of the grade, but I am proud of the work I devoted. From that experience, I learned how to adjust my study skills and the importance of understanding material before moving on to new topics. This gave me practice for the quick, rigorous nature of PA school.

Ways to Rephrase:

- What was your most difficult class in undergrad?
- What is the hardest class you've ever taken?
- What non-science undergraduate course will benefit you most in PA school?
- How would you describe your overall academic performance?

9. YOU ARE A PA. YOU ARE AT A BASEBALL GAME AND THE WOMAN IN FRONT OF YOU HAS A SUSPICIOUS MOLE YOU SUSPECT COULD BE MELANOMA. WHAT DO YOU DO?

This is a tough situation. It comes down to what you consider your responsibilities as a healthcare provider. Do you have a duty to people who are not technically your patients because you have medical knowledge? Or do you avoid interfering in someone's life and possibly causing unnecessary fear?

There are so many ways to approach this situation, but consider your personality and comfort level. Here are some options:

- Do nothing. If you don't feel comfortable approaching a stranger about a medical issue while at a sporting event, that's understandable. It could be unwanted advice and they may not respond favorably. But consider how you would feel afterwards and if you would have regrets about saying nothing.
- Just tell them! If you see something potentially harmful, it may be your instinct to go for it and let them know, especially if you know it will linger if you don't. You may face rejection, but knowing you tried may be worth it.
- Approach the situation slowly. Try to strike up a friendly conversation and get to know the person. If the opportunity arises and you feel comfortable, gently suggest they visit their primary care or a dermatologist. It's a great opportunity to explain your job and training as a PA to validate your observations.

When practicing and studying for these types of situations with many options, consider all possibilities and weigh why you would choose one over the other. I can't choose what the right answer would be for you.

10. YOU ARE A PA. A PATIENT ON YOUR SCHEDULE INSISTS ON SEEING AN MD. HOW DO YOU HANDLE IT?

This is a common occurrence when working as a PA, and you're likely to see this firsthand while shadowing. If not observed during your time, ask a PA how they feel when patients request to see the doctor and how they handle those situations.

This question is important because you have to address this without being offended or becoming defensive. If you are a PA, this will happen! Part of the reason stems from patients who don't fully understand what a PA is, or how we fit into healthcare. This presents an opportunity to exhibit good bedside manner, and also explain the professional responsibilities of a PA.

When a patient is apprehensive about seeing a PA, it's best to introduce yourself and answer questions about their reservations. At the end of the day, it's the patient's choice whether or not they see a PA or physician, but they must understand their preferences may not be met right away. If a patient is on the PA's schedule, it's possible the physician's schedule is too full that day for additional patients, or they may be out of the office. At that point, the patient may reschedule or make a follow-up appointment with the physician.

What NOT To Do: Become aggressive, demanding, or rude. You must keep your composure, and exhibit professionalism. If presented in a roleplaying scenario, the "patient" may exhibit anger or frustration, but you cannot respond with your own.

Ways to Rephrase:

- How would you feel if a patient refused to see you because you're a PA?
- How can you earn respect as a PA?

11. A PATIENT IS NOT PROFICIENT IN ENGLISH, AND YOU ARE UNFAMILIAR WITH THEIR LANGUAGE. HOW CAN YOU ASSIST?

Also known as "Are you a problem solver?" That's what this question is alluding to. Are you able and willing to take an extra step to guarantee your patients receive the best care? Working in medicine, you will likely be required to accommodate for patients, and language barriers can present real issues.

You will encounter this working as a PA. I recently had a patient who did not speak English as their first language. As I was explaining the need to keep a lesion covered with a Band-aid, the patient's mom was nodding her head. After a few moments, I started to wonder if she actually understood. I asked, "Do you know what a Band-aid is?" After being direct, she responded with no. That was simple to remedy because I showed her a Band-aid to give her understanding.

You're not expected to know every law pertaining to interpreters or using family members to translate as this can vary between facility and state, but you do need the ability to think on your toes. Technology has made language barriers less of an obstacle, but in medicine you need an accurate picture of the patient's needs and a way to provide instructions the patient can understand. Using an app like Google Translate could be an option, but there may be questions to how accurate the translation is. When I see patients who speak a different language, I provide handouts on their diagnoses and written instructions so a family member can help at home. I wouldn't be surprised if features are put into EMRs in the future to make these experiences easier for both the provider and the patient.

If you've personally experienced this, it's a great chance to tell your story. Or if you are bilingual, you may have observed family members in similar situations, so you can relate and may have better tips for what is practically helpful.

12. WHAT IS SOMETHING DIFFICULT YOU HAVE HAD TO DISCUSS WITH SOMEONE?

If you're going into healthcare, be prepared for the difficult discussions, and this could be with anyone including patients and their families, co-workers or your supervising physician, or even your own friends and family members. It may not be in a healthcare setting, but consider the experience you already have before you get to PA school.

Working in healthcare, you won't always make everyone happy, which can lead to these difficult discussions. Even simple conversations I had as a CNA, such as explaining why a patient is on a diabetic or low sodium diet and unable to enjoy their favorite foods, were unpleasant. Now as a PA, I must discuss treatment options for skin cancer and sometimes patients don't prefer any of my available options.

It's essential to have these tough conversations in a way patients will understand. Try to think of a specific example you could share during your interview, even if it wasn't with a patient. It could be a situation with a friend or co-worker as well. Many times, addressing conflict tends to feel difficult, so that is a good place to start.

Ways to Rephrase:

- Have you ever had to share bad news?

13. DESCRIBE A SITUATION YOU HAVE HAD WITH A DIFFICULT PATIENT.

My least favorite answer to this question is, "I've never had a difficult patient." What?!? It blows me away to hear this during a mock interview. If you've had any type of patient interaction, you've experienced a "difficult" patient. We've all had difficult patients (and maybe even been one at some point)!

Interpretation of the question depends on the person and your specific experiences. My first instinct of "difficult" is someone who is rude, mean, or hard to handle. From mock interviews, I've found that some people attack this question with a different perspective of the patient encounter that was just difficult to handle, such as a patient dying from cancer or a non-compliant patient you try to help, but with failed attempts.

If a question is phrased generally, it's up to you to analyze and address it. Don't get hung up on what kind of "difficult" the question is asking about. Focus on your first instinct and pull out the overarching lesson from that patient encounter. Why was this difficult or important to you? How will it affect future patient interactions?

Ways to Rephrase:

- Discuss a situation with a patient that had a significant impact on you.

14. HOW DO YOU DEAL WITH HIGH STRESS SITUATIONS? GIVE AN EXAMPLE.

Obviously as a PA student, and as a PA, you will face high stress situations. So why would you be asked this question? The interviewer seeks assurance of your previous experience with stress, so when faced with situations in the future, you'll have coping mechanisms to handle them adequately.

Your examples do not have to be academic or clinical in nature, but can come from life experiences. Here are possible examples to help jog your memory:

- Having multiple finals while working during undergrad
- Overcommitting yourself to too many activities or commitments

- Being the first person to witness an accident or injury
- Dealing with an angry person and diffusing the situation
- Making a mistake and having to rectify it

When giving your example, explain what happened, but focus on your response to the situation. During difficult times, I tend to pause, take a deep breath, then look at the little things that need done to fix the problem. With studying, that means breaking down each concept and determining focus areas to get my studying done. I can accomplish this more efficiently in a quiet, isolated location. I also like to talk things out with a friend or family member. Your response in a stressful situation may look differently from mine, but you want to be both personal and practical with your answer.

Bonus Points: Relate your answer back specifically to how your stress coping mechanisms will help you succeed in PA school and be a better student. Stress in PA school is unavoidable, and sometimes you just have to cry it out, but that's not the best way to handle it. On a daily basis, you need to find a reliable method to deal with the stressors you will inevitably face. Working out is a common answer, as well as a healthy way to blow off steam. Maybe you go for a walk, play with your dog, meditate, or whatever your strategy, reassure the admissions committee that PA school won't be too much for you to deal with. Maybe your class will have a massage therapist who can relieve everyone's stress!

Ways to Rephrase:

- How do you handle stress?
- Have you ever been stressed out?
- Discuss a high stress situation you have had in the past.
- How will you handle the stress of PA school?

- What is the most stressful part of your current job?
- What coping mechanisms have you developed for dealing with stress?

15. TELL ME ABOUT A TIME YOU USED TEAMWORK TO SOLVE A PROBLEM.

By now, I hope you have a firm grasp on how important teamwork is for PA school and practicing in healthcare. The experience requirements show good communication is crucial for providing quality care for patients, but your example doesn't necessarily have to come from the healthcare realm.

An example from your education can show that you'll be the type of PA student who will work well with others and problem solve without the need to involve faculty if you have a trivial issue. Many group projects may present conflicts that must be resolved to ensure the work gets done in a timely fashion.

Once you've shared your experience and described your role, the problem, and what you did to solve it, come full circle to emphasize the direct connection to how this lesson will help you succeed in PA school as a team player.

Ways to Rephrase:

- Do you prefer to work with others or by yourself?
- What is the most important factor between a PA and supervising physician?

16. DO YOU THINK IT'S MORE IMPORTANT TO GET PATIENTS SEEN OR SPEND TIME WITH PATIENTS?

This can be a tough question for the typical perfectionist, "Type A" personality that tends to describe many PA school applicants. And it's a tough one for me! I value efficiency, but there's a happy medium between making sure patients are seen in a timely fashion, while giving them adequate attention.

If you've worked with patients, you're likely familiar with "the talker." What started as a simple follow-up for a rash (that has completely resolved) somehow turns into a 10 minute conversation about the patient's sister's new roof. What? How did we get here? I've come to realize sometimes patients just need a person to listen, and it's great to be that person for them when you can.

On the flip side, part of the job description as a PA is to see and treat patients. There are many steps involved: getting the patient checked in, verifying insurance, taking a history, review of systems, physical examination, discussion of treatment options, writing prescriptions, and finally you must complete the note! Overall, it's more important to spend time with patients, but maintain a good understanding of how to efficiently accomplish the steps listed to stay on schedule if possible. A waiting patient is typically not a happy patient.

Ways to Rephrase:

- If a patient is late, should they still be seen?
- How much time should be allotted to spend with each patient?

17. DESCRIBE YOUR WORK ETHIC.

It takes a strong work ethic to complete the requirements for PA school, and it's definitely not easy to take classes while trying to gain experience, shadow, and volunteer. The schools expect a lot from you to earn a spot in their program.

PA school is hard. If you don't already know that, let me be the first to tell you (and you may want to talk to some other PA students before you apply). It's essential to prove to your interviewers that you have developed time management skills to survive grad school, and that you know what to expect once you get there.

Even though this question just says "describe," think about rephrasing the prompt to "Tell me about a time that you have displayed your work ethic." This will help to elicit a story and make your answer stronger.

Ways to Rephrase:

- How are your time management skills?
- Did you work while getting your prerequisites?
- Would you say you're a hard worker?
- What did you have to sacrifice to get to this interview?
- Give an example of a goal you reached and tell how you achieved it.
- Where do you get your motivation?
- What would your best friend say about you?
- Tell me about a situation when you had to push yourself.

18. WOULD YOU ACCEPT A FACEBOOK FRIEND REQUEST FROM A PATIENT?

Social media, the internet, and technology are integrating into health-care and can't be ignored at this point. If you haven't heard of "Dr. Google" or been tempted to Facebook stalk a patient, don't worry, it will happen. But where do you draw the line?

This is not only addressing how technology affects your career, but also a question of professionalism and what you view as appropriate interactions between a provider and a patient. Personally, I am not going to accept a friend request from a patient I do not know outside of caring for them from a medical standpoint. It's not quite enough to say you wouldn't accept the friend request, but take this opportunity to share your thoughts on technology's role in medicine. And to go further, how do you see technology affecting healthcare in the future?

At the end of the day, it's important to maintain a professional relationship with patients as their provider, not their friend. Even a Facebook friend.

Ways to Rephrase:

- How has technology affected healthcare?
- How do you predict technology will affect healthcare in the future?
- Do you think providers should be Facebook friends with patients?

19. HOW WOULD YOU FEEL IN PA SCHOOL IF YOU WERE DOING POORLY IN A SUBJECT THAT YOU EXCELLED IN DURING UNDERGRAD?

The point of this question is to see if you understand the likelihood of struggles during PA school. Everyone has courses that were more difficult for some reason or another, but part of what makes PA school coursework tough is the volume of information in a short time period. It can be hard to keep up and overwhelming at times.

I'll use anatomy as an example. If you thought there were a ton of structures to learn during undergrad level anatomy, graduate school takes it to a whole new level. There's so much more! Every single structure has a name, function, and reason you need to know it. I did awesome in my summer anatomy course, but on the first test in PA school I received a C. That was disheartening, but with the next test two weeks away, I didn't have much time to make adjustments.

There were two choices: study the same way I did for the first test (which clearly didn't work) or ask for help. There was no time to feel discouraged or disappointed. After reaching out to the professor, our teaching assistants, and finding a group of classmates to study with, I adjusted my study skills and passed with an A. Acknowledge the rigor of PA school as something you are ready for and show you can adapt without letting it get you down.

Ways to Rephrase:

- Do you ever get angry or frustrated?
- How do you handle disappointment?

20. DEFINE PROFESSIONALISM.

Let's start with Webster's definition of professionalism:

Professionalism: the conduct, aims, or qualities that characterize or mark a profession or a professional person

I feel like that doesn't give much direction or specificity, so here's the broken-down definition for "English Language Learners:"

Professionalism: the skill, good judgment, and polite behavior that is expected from a person who is trained to do a job well

That definition gives a bit more information. Now apply these characteristics of "skill, good judgment, and polite behavior" to working in the medical field. Skill is required to execute procedures correctly and with confidence. As a PA, good judgement is necessary when making decisions about patient care and knowing when to consult a supervising physician for assistance. In any situation, politeness is beneficial. In your own words, define professionalism.

Think about why this concept is important for you to grasp. As a PA, or anyone working in medicine for that matter, it is essential to consistently exhibit the highest level of professionalism with patients and co-workers. In order to embrace a characteristic, you should be able to define it, preferably in your own terms.

My Definition: To me, professionalism is a quality all people should strive for in any job or activity. Professionalism consists of treating everyone with kindness and respect, and doing so in a way that earns the respect of others. It also means having confidence, but knowing when to seek assistance to ensure outcomes are of the highest quality.

Bonus Points: Think of a specific time you have displayed professionalism, or seen this quality in a colleague or PA. Describe exactly what stood out about this person or situation that required an attitude of professionalism and how it was exemplified.

Ways to Rephrase:

- What does professionalism mean to you?
- What does it mean to portray yourself in a professional manner?
- Tell me about someone you've worked with who exhibited professionalism.

21. IF YOU WERE TO WIN THE LOTTERY, WHAT WOULD YOU DO? WOULD YOU STILL WANT TO BE A PA?

Is money your main motivator for becoming a PA? That's what this question comes down to. You may think it sounds silly, but PAs typically have good salaries, and it may be easy for some people to think, "I can go to school for two years and come out with a six-figure salary." Sounds good, right?

If you've done your homework, you've realized it's not that simple. Between the requirements and cost of school, it's a huge commitment you hope will pay off financially at some point. Now if you didn't necessarily have to work (assuming you didn't completely blow your lottery money), would you really want to be a PA? I hope so!

There's no right answer to this question, and the only wrong answer is saying you would no longer pursue the PA route. That implies you are only doing it for the money and not because you are passionate about medicine and helping patients. It's reasonable to do something fun with your money, like get a new car or go on a crazy vacation! The freedom to choose your position that would come with winning the lottery would be awesome.

Ways to Rephrase:

- Do you realize you'll make less money than a physician?
- Should PAs be reimbursed at the same rate as physicians?
- If PAs made $20,000 a year, would you still want to be a PA?

22. GIVE AN EXAMPLE OF A SITUATION IN WHICH YOU EXCEEDED EXPECTATIONS.

These questions are trying to ascertain what your character is really like and learn more about the strength of your work ethic and response to certain situations. You can use work or personal examples for this type of question.

I think of a day recently when my supervising physician came down with a stomach bug. She made it through morning clinic, but was seriously struggling to make it through the afternoon. I stepped in between seeing my own patients to help with notes, and ultimately ended up staying late and seeing her last patients in order for her to go home. Is there a time you've picked up a shift to help someone else out? Or given a friend a ride when you really had something else to do?

Ways to Rephrase:

- Tell me about a time that you surprised yourself.
- Discuss a time that you had to help someone else out.

23. TELL ME ABOUT A TIME YOU BROKE THE RULES.

We've all broken the rules at some point, right? It's just not fun to own up to it. Even if you speed to get to work on time or don't stop completely at the stop sign, you're a rule breaker.

I actually hate breaking rules, and I tend to err on the side of being over cautious, but it still happens occasionally. This question is seeing if you can honestly own up to your mistakes. Schools are looking for candidates that will admit to making a mistake because it will inevitably happen in your future career.

If you have any major red flags on your application, use this opportunity to address them. I'm talking academic probation or misdemeanors. Basically anything you had to explain on your application. Whatever happened, the most important aspect is explaining what lesson you learned from that situation and how it made you a better person overall. That should translate into the type of PA you will become.

Ways to Rephrase:

- What is the worst mistake you have ever made?

24. HOW HAS YOUR INTERVIEW EXPERIENCE BEEN TODAY?

It's important to show schools you want to attend their programs, and that you've been paying attention throughout your interview experience. Be able to discuss what you learned about the program, what surprised you, and what impressed you during your time at the interview.

Throughout your entire interview, you should be trying to portray enthusiasm and confidence in your dedication to attend. Take this opportunity to reflect on the best parts of your day, and complement the program on their accomplishments. Also, feel free to use this chance to confirm they are a top choice for you, and the interview should support that.

On the flip side, what happens if you had a terrible interview experience? Honesty is the best policy, but avoid insulting the program in any way. I would recommend keeping it short and sweet if the interview was not what you were expecting or changed your opinion of the program, and simply state that you've had a fine day and look forward to their decision.

Ways to Rephrase:

- Did you learn anything new about our program today?
- What stood out to you most about your experience at the interview today?
- Tell me about the last person who interviewed you.
- What were the names of the interviewers you already met today?

25. IS THERE ANYTHING ELSE I NEED TO KNOW ABOUT YOU?

This is it! This question indicates the interview is almost over and you made it out alive. Don't lose this opportunity to bring up anything you haven't had the chance to address yet. Particularly information that is not on your application, as you're being given the chance to share something about yourself. Be personal with your response, and share an interesting fact if you feel that you've covered all of your bases during the interview. This is your last chance to make an impression.

If you feel you've said everything you needed to say, this is also a perfect time to inform the program of your interests in going there. How will they know they're your top choice if you don't tell them? There's no shame in confirming your interest and being direct when telling your interviewers you want to attend their program. I did this and I think it paid off. Also, be sure to thank them for the interview invite and the experience you had while there.

Ways to Rephrase:

- Tell me something that's not on your application.
- Tell me something you've never told anyone else.
- If you had a memoir, what would it be called?
- When you leave today what one thing will you wish you could have told us about yourself?

CHAPTER 6
ETHICAL QUESTIONS

Ethical questions, which can bring up controversial topics, tend to scare applicants for fear they might say the "wrong" thing. These types of questions do come down to "right" or "wrong," but typically there are variations involved. Your version of what's considered "right" may depend on your personal beliefs and experiences, but usually the "wrong" notion is clear. For example, is cheating ever okay? Nope. If you witness an event that could harm a patient, should you ignore it? Nope.

While it's easy to know what you shouldn't do, determining the best course of action can be more difficult. When in doubt, go with your best instincts. You need to take a solid stance and explain your opinion.

1. DISCUSS A CURRENT MEDICAL ETHICS ISSUES.

There are so many though! This is an example of an extremely open-ended prompt. If you're presented with this type of question without being asked for specifics, it is up to your interpretation where you go with your answer. You could approach it from discussing a current event or an ethical dilemma you have already encountered while gaining your experience. Here are some topics to consider:

- Physician-assisted suicide
- Opioid epidemic
- Patients going to other countries for risky surgeries
- Birth control usage in pediatric patients
- Abortion as a provider if against their beliefs
- Speaking poorly about patients when out of the room or when the patient is under anesthesia
- Using Google or Facebook to look up a patient
- Having to tell a patient's partner about HIV or STI status
- Universal health insurance
- Social Security availability for health costs

I would recommend choosing an issue, stating the reason it's controversial and why people may disagree, and then making your case on the issue. Ultimately, I can't tell you how to answer this question because it's likely our opinions differ! This is not the place for interjecting your own political views, and when discussing a hot topic, remain objective to show you will not be a judgmental provider as a PA.

Ways to Rephrase:

- Is it ethical to treat your family members? Would you do it?
- Tell me about a time you had to make an ethical decision.

2. IF A PATIENT HAS AIDS, WILL YOU STILL TREAT THEM?

This is a pretty blunt ethical question, but consider the ways you could put a spin on this. The interviewer is trying to determine if you have any bias that will affect how you treat patients. This can be difficult if you aren't familiar with HIV/AIDS because there is significant stigma surrounding the topic. While AIDS is a terrible and communicable disease, it doesn't mean patients with AIDS should receive any different treatment. At the end of the day, as someone working in medicine, you must be willing to have a non-judgmental attitude and a disposition that will allow you to treat everyone the same.

I see HIV patients as a dermatology PA, and they require procedures or biopsies just like other patients. I'm as cautious as I would be with any patient, and regardless of the alert on their chart, I don't avoid doing procedures due to fear of becoming infected with HIV.

If you read this question and have an instant feeling of fear or apprehension, seek someone who works closely with HIV patients and have a conversation about their job. You'll find it's not as scary as you think, and your preconceived notions are likely incorrect. In the "Ways to Rephrase," we bring up the issue of who deserves to know about a communicable disease status. Many states have laws regarding this, and as a healthcare provider, you may be required to report a positive test so partners can be notified and receive appropriate testing and treatment.

Ways to Rephrase:

- You have diagnosed a patient with HIV, and they do not want to tell their partner. What do you do?
- What would you do if you diagnose a patient with syphilis, but he doesn't plan to tell his girlfriend?

3. YOU ARE A PA. YOUR SUPERVISING MD ASKS YOU TO ADMINISTER A MEDICATION TO A PATIENT. YOU DO NOT AGREE WITH HIS DECISION AND FEEL IT COULD HARM THE PATIENT. WHAT DO YOU DO?

This is getting into ethics of what you are responsible for as a PA, and you need to consider why this question is asked. The main point is whether you understand what autonomy as a PA means, regardless of requests from your supervising physician. This question also explores your understanding of the relationship between PAs and their supervising physicians.

As any medical provider, your main concern is patient safety above all else. It's part of the Hippocratic oath. You can seek assistance from your supervising physician, but if they are unavailable, the decision comes to you. In this scenario, if you don't feel something benefits the patient, you should have enough confidence in your knowledge as a PA to make a well-informed decision. At the end of the day, if you follow through with an action you disagree with and harm a patient, it's your license on the line.

You should feel confident enough to have a conversation with your supervising physician about any concerns. They serve as a teacher and advisor, not a dictator. It's possible you don't understand something about the patient's current status, and you may learn from inquiring about the case. It's also possible for the physician to make a mistake. Maybe they told you the wrong medication or the wrong patient! That's where the checks and balance system of the PA/MD relationship is beneficial for the quality of patient care. Your interviewer needs to see that you will stand up for yourself and your patients if necessary. So here are some steps to consider in your approach:

- Do your research on the patient by reviewing the chart and speaking with the nurse and the patient.

- Try to get in touch with your supervising physician for clarification.
- If unable to get in touch with your supervising physician, make your decision based on what's best for the patient.
- Document your actions thoroughly.

What NOT to say: The incorrect answer is blindly doing whatever your supervising physician tells you to do. That is irresponsible and makes it seem like you don't have a thorough understanding of the role of a PA.

4. YOU SEE A CO-WORKER TAKING MEDICATION FROM THE DISPENSE CART AND PUTTING IT IN HER BAG. WHAT DO YOU DO?

This sounds sketchy, right? This is a tough situation to be in as the observer. Let's breakdown why this action could be inappropriate.

- Endangering a patient by potentially taking their prescribed medication
- Taking controlled substances, which could indicate a drug abuse problem. If there is a drug problem, is that worker capable of doing their job responsibly?
- Stealing from the hospital or clinic
- Disregard for rules and willingness to commit an unethical act

While it would absolutely stink to be in that situation, if you witness a questionable act, you are now involved. This is your chance to demonstrate your strong ethics, and willingness to take action. There are several options to consider.

You can go first to the co-worker and give them an opportunity to explain, or you can approach a supervisor without saying anything to the co-worker and let them know what you observed. If you don't get a reasonable explanation from your co-worker, or even if you do, it's not a bad idea to go to your supervisor. This is analogous to a cheating scenario.

What NOT to say: That you would do nothing. No one wants to be a snitch, but if you know something unethical is going on (especially in an interview setting), you need to be the person to step up and do something about it. Your moral compass would be compromised if you turn a blind eye to inappropriate actions or behaviors.

Ways to Rephrase:

- If you found out a classmate had old copies of exams, what would you do?

5. YOU ARE IN A SURGERY AND THE ANESTHESIOLOGIST BEGINS TO MAKE INAPPROPRIATE COMMENTS ABOUT THE PATIENT ONCE THEY ARE ASLEEP. WHAT DO YOU DO IN THIS SITUATION?

You may have actually heard about this in the news at some point. The occasional story of a patient who finds a phone recording of the surgeon cracking jokes about their weight or appearance after the procedure emerges occasionally. Not good!

Let's complicate this situation one step further and pretend you're a PA student on clinical rotations. Yikes. This goes back to to advocating for your patients. There are a few steps you may consider taking:

- Say something directly to the surgeon to let them know

you feel uncomfortable. Could this affect your grade? It's possible, but you may remind the surgeon that patients deserve respect at all times, even under anesthesia.

- Let someone else know, such as a supervisor, another surgeon, or your clinical rotation coordinator. If you wouldn't feel comfortable speaking directly to the surgeon, make sure someone knows about your concerns regarding the behavior in the OR.
- Nothing, aka wrong answer. In medicine, and life in general, if something inappropriate is happening, be willing to take action. This applies even at the student level because what you witness might just be the tip of the iceberg.

Ways to Rephrase:

- You're in an OR and have suspicions that the surgeon may be intoxicated. What do you do?

6. YOU HAVE AN ELDERLY PATIENT WHO NEEDS TO STAY AT THE HOSPITAL FOR OVERNIGHT OBSERVATION. THE PATIENT IS REFUSING, BUT THE PATIENT'S SON STATES THE PATIENT HAS DEMENTIA AND IS INCAPABLE OF MAKING MEDICAL DECISIONS. THE PATIENT'S SON WANTS THE PATIENT ADMITTED. WHAT DO YOU DO?

Yikes, we're getting into some dicey stuff. As a medical provider, you try to make decisions in the best interest of the patient, but you also have to consider the patient's desires. That changes if the patient is unable to independently make sound, reasonable decisions.

This is discussed more in the psychiatric realm, but sometimes patients wish to leave "against medical advice," or A.M.A. As a medical provider, your responsibility is to make sure the patient understands the risks of leaving without proper care. Put your communication skills to work, but at the end of the day, you may not be able to convince the patient to do what you think is in their best interest. Keep in mind, patients have a say in their care, or lack of care in this instance.

In some states there are options to put a legal hold on a patient so they are unable to leave the hospital, but these can be lengthy and difficult to obtain and may not be realistic in all situations. You're not expected to know all of the specifics for your state, but you could mention you would take the initiative to further research these options if faced with this situation.

7. YOU ARE LEAVING FOR THE DAY AND REALIZE YOU GAVE A PATIENT MEDICATION THEY ARE ALLERGIC TO. WHAT DO YOU DO?

No matter what your career is, you will make mistakes. It's human nature. No one is perfect. But how you address that mistake says a lot about who you are as a person.

We'll go back to the fact that as a medical provider, your goal is to do no harm to your patients. Fortunately, for this situation, there are many checks and balances in place between electronic medical records (EMRs) and pharmacies to prevent this problem from occurring. Despite these attempts, things slip through the cracks, and there is the possibility a patient may end up with unintended medication.

The worst thing you can do in this situation is nothing. You made a mistake, so humble yourself and fix it. You have an ethical and professional responsibility to do everything in your power to keep your patient safe. Here's what I would do:

- Call the patient immediately to inquire if they picked up or took the medication yet. Explain the mistake to the patient and instruct them to not pick up or take the medication. If they have already ingested the medicine, I would encourage them to go to an urgent care or ER if they have a true allergy that would cause anaphylaxis.

- Call the pharmacy. Verify the status of the medication and whether the patient picked it up. Cancel the prescription and let the pharmacist know about the allergy so an alert can be put on the patient's records.

At this point, you are thinking you've covered your bases and done all you can. But then your interviewer says, "What if you can't get in touch with the patient?"

Well, that's certainly a possibility. In that case, do all you can to follow every lead. Contact every number available for that patient, leave messages if necessary (typically, you want to avoid leaving personal healthcare information on voicemail due to HIPAA, but in a possible life or death situation for my patient, I would be letting them know to NOT take the medication prescribed and call immediately), leave your cell phone number and multiple ways to reach you. Make every effort, and that's all you can do.

Ways to Rephrase:

- A patient comes in for follow-up and you realize they were prescribed the wrong medication, but one with a similar name. What do you do?
- You are working as a PA. You realize your nurse sent in the wrong medication for a patient. What do you do?
- You realize you sent an adult dosage of medication for a child. What do you do?
- You've prescribed an antibiotic, but after the patient leaves you realize there's a contraindication with one of their other medications. What do you do?
- A patient calls back for their culture results, and you

realize the test was never sent in. The sample is no longer good. What do you do?

- When is honesty not the best policy?

8. YOU ARE SEEING A JEHOVAH'S WITNESS PATIENT. DUE TO RELIGIOUS BELIEFS, HE/SHE DOES NOT ACCEPT BLOOD TRANSFUSIONS, BUT IT COULD BE LIFE-SAVING. WHAT DO YOU DO?

Religious beliefs + medicine = messy territory.

I would tell you to catch up on *Grey's Anatomy* and *House* since they tend to cover these types of situations, but they often don't make the most ethical decisions and end up causing more problems.

It is part of the Jehovah's Witness belief system to not accept blood transfusions for any reason, no matter how dire the situation or if it is potentially life-saving. That can be frustrating for a medical provider trying to provide the best care in order to save a life. Once again, this comes down to patient respect and the fact that ultimately, the patient can make decisions about their own care.

It is reasonable to have an honest conversation with the patient or their family about the risks and benefits of accepting versus denying the transfusion, but at the end of the day the power to make the decision is in their hands. It gets more complicated in the case of children, and there are cases where courts have gotten involved and ordered that minors DO receive a transfusion despite their parent's wishes. Feel free to Google "Jehovah's Witness blood transfusion case" if you want to read more on this because it is quite interesting.

After presenting the options, it's still your job to do everything you can to save the patient, even if the treatment options left aren't your preference, so make that clear in your interview. You don't need to identify specific interventions, but be willing to work with your team to support the patient's wishes.

Ways to Rephrase:

- A child is brought in with injuries from falling out of a tree at a friend's house. His parents are out of town. After evaluation, it is determined that he requires a blood transfusion. Before giving the transfusion, you find a card in his pocket stating he is Jehovah's Witness and to not give blood transfusions. The procedure would save his life, but no parents are present. What do you do?

9. YOU ARE A PA AND YOU PRESCRIBED BIRTH CONTROL PILLS FOR A 13-YEAR-OLD. THE PATIENT'S MOTHER IS ANGRY ABOUT THIS DECISION. WHAT DO YOU SAY?

Angry parents add a whole new level to the conflict of ethical scenarios. This question is not asking about your thoughts and opinions on whether a 13-year-old should take birth control. It's asking how you would deal with a parent questioning your decisions, which we would hope you made in the best interest of the patient.

The birth control dilemma is difficult because some of the regulations surrounding this issue will depend on state laws, and you shouldn't be expected to understand those fully, but acknowledge that they exist. Oftentimes, any information pertaining to a patient's sexual health (including pregnancy, STIs, HIV) is excluded from the requirement to disclose patient information to parents or guardians if a child is a minor or under 18. Mental health and substance abuse also fall under this umbrella. This means the patient can share concerns without the fear or obligation of parental consent, and you are free to treat these patients.

As a complicating factor, most often, the minor is on their parent's insurance so when they pick up the contraceptive, the parent will likely find out. That makes parents question your involvement.

The best way to approach this question is to discuss how you would first want to understand the state laws surrounding this issue, what you are held to under HIPAA, and what you are obligated to tell the parents. At this point, you may not be able to freely share with the parent if the child asked you not to, but as the healthcare provider, you may help facilitate a conversation if both parties are willing. It's important to keep your cool and show you can be a problem solver and good communicator, even in a tense situation.

I personally see this in my job since birth control is a treatment for acne. Even if a 17-year-old comes in without a parent and we are discussing starting oral contraceptives "for acne" (sometimes there is a double reason the patient is interested), I encourage the patient to involve their parents in the discussion. I explain the complications of insurance and the pharmacy that may inform their parents of the medication. I offer to be present and lead the discussion to make it less uncomfortable and ensure we're all on the same page.

10. WHAT WOULD YOU DO IF YOU HIT YOUR NEIGHBOR'S DOG?

First of all, if this has actually happened to you (as either the driver or the neighbor), I am so sorry. This is not a fun situation to be in for either person. This question looks at your morality to see if you can own up to making a mistake and how you would handle it.

There are many ways to address this issue - speak with the neighbor immediately, call your neighbor, take the dog to the vet for help. The wrong answer here is to do nothing and drive away. That is ethically just not okay. If you make a mistake, even a terribly sad one, you have to own up to it and attempt to make retributions.

Ways to Rephrase:

- What would you do if you hit a car in a parking lot? You're unsure of the owner.

CHAPTER 7

MULTIPLE MINI INTERVIEW (MMI) QUESTIONS

I'll be honest, MMI is my least favorite interview type because it is more difficult to prepare for. They tend to be completely random, and don't typically allow a direct chance to address the reasons you want to become a PA. MMI has you do more "show" than "tell" in an attempt to evaluate your personality.

The prompts range from routine interview questions to ethical situations, critical thinking scenarios, or acting stations with standardized patients. The use of scenarios assesses various qualities, such as empathy, decision making, and communication skills. If you can identify the characteristic each particular scenario is focused on, your response will be stronger. There are not necessarily "right or wrong" answers to scenarios because the purpose is to evaluate the attributes and personal characteristics you would exhibit as a PA. The best way to succeed in an MMI is to practice "thinking out loud," which shows the interviewer your ability to consider different possibilities, form an opinion, and defend it. This will be demonstrated in the following question examples.

Part of MMI practice is making your answers fit the allotted time.

It's not crucial to talk for the full 5 minutes, but take enough time to explain your position fully without running out of time. While going through practice prompts, use timers to monitor your time management. Set a timer for 2 minutes to review the prompt and organize your thoughts, and then reset at 5 minutes for your answer. Address all parts of the prompt, as leaving information out is a common mistake.

1. IF YOU WERE A TREE, WHAT KIND WOULD YOU BE AND WHY?

You're already hoping you don't get this question, and I'm right there with you. The most common first instinct is, "How am I supposed to talk about a tree for 5 minutes?" I've had one person in a mock interview who rocked this answer, spoke for the entire 5 minutes, and he was accepted! Creativity goes a long way in MMI.

These off-the-wall, wacky questions are designed to throw you off, uncover your imagination, and see what connections you make. You can substitute just about anything for "tree" in this prompt. In this instance, choose an object/adjective, relate it to yourself, and explain why with examples. Here are some examples with trees:

- Redwood - Strong roots and supports other trees
- Evergreen - Stay consistent through all seasons
- Bonsai tree - A tree of respect and knowledge because they grow over a long time
- Palm tree - Loves the beach, but withstands strong winds of hurricanes
- Pine tree - Consistently produces seeds to spread and share with surrounding area

Look for specific characteristics to discuss that relate to personality traits you offer, and expand on those. For the Redwood example, discuss your tendency to be a great study partner because of your dedication and positive attitude, and back it up with details.

What not to do: Walk in and say, "I would be an apple tree because I love apples." And that's it. You must be more creative and use the allotted time wisely. Take the experiences from the Chapter 13 worksheets and work those in to your answer.

Ways to Rephrase:

- If you were a color, what color would you be, and why?
- If you were dressing up for a halloween party for kids, what would you dress up as, and why?
- If you were a car, what kind would you be, and why?
- If you were a candy bar, what kind would you be, and why?
- If you could have any super power, what would you choose, and why?
- If you were an animal, what would you be, and why?

2. WHAT THREE PEOPLE, LIVING OR DEAD, WOULD YOU INVITE TO DINNER? WHAT WOULD YOU SERVE THEM?

This could be a fun question, but it can stump people. There is no "right" answer to this question! I've heard anyone from family members or friends to celebrities or the president. There is no profound way to answer, just go with your gut. Choose individuals you would like to meet, have more time with, or learn something from. Taylor Swift would definitely be one of my three because I would love to meet her, and crab cakes would be my main course. In order to talk about this for more than 30 seconds, go beyond stating who you are inviting, but why you chose those people. What are you hoping to get out of the conversation? How would they interact with each other?

This question demonstrates a common feature of MMI because the prompt has two distinct questions: who would be invited and what would be served. When given a prompt, address **all** parts of the question. It's not uncommon to feel flustered trying to come up with the guests, and completely forget to address the dinner portion. When you choose your dinner menu, explain why. Is it your favorite food or something you cook well? Is there sentimental value? Give your interviewer the opportunity to learn about you, your background, and interests through this question.

Ways to Rephrase:

- Name three role models and why you look up to them.
- What characteristics make a person a good role model?
- If you could spend a day with one person, who would you choose, and why? What would you do?
- What would you do if you were president for a day?

3. HELP THIS STUDENT COMPLETE THE FOLLOWING TASK...

Scenarios are common in MMI, and there might be a person waiting in the room that you have to direct. A task evaluates your communication skills to determine if you can effectively give directions. Throughout these scenarios, you cannot be too detailed in your instructions.

To practice, start thinking through every step of your mundane tasks. The ones you normally don't have to think about at all. When you brush your teeth, think about picking up the toothpaste tube in your left hand, turning the lid to the left to remove it and setting it on the counter, then squeezing the tube to dispense a pea size amount of toothpaste onto the brush end of your toothbrush. How would you explain the things you do to someone who has never done them, particularly if you aren't able to show the steps?

It seems silly, but paying attention to detail is important for working in healthcare. Once you start instructing patients on how to use medications, you'll need those communication skills. Occasionally, I'll have a follow-up patient tell me they are not doing any better with the medication I prescribed (usually a cream since I work in dermatology). It's amazing how many people wash topical medicine off after applying it! I'm much better now at emphasizing the instructions of leaving cream on after applied. Although it seems like common sense, I've learned that others think differently.

Ways to Rephrase:

- Give directions for putting on a pair of gloves.
- Give instructions for making a peanut butter and jelly sandwich.
- While sitting back to back, tell the person in the room how to draw a tree.
- Explain how to make a paper airplane.
- Help the patient in the room fill out their intake form. (Once in the room, you find that the patient is homeless, cannot read, and does not know much of the information.)

4. INTERPRET THE GRAPH DISPLAYED IN THE ROOM.

Can you analyze data? That's the purpose of asking you to interpret a graph or test results. This should not require medical knowledge, but just the basics you've learned from your math and science courses and information you used on the GRE.

Use the "think out loud" technique for this type of station. Show your thought process of working through the graph or problem instead of walking in and jumping right to your answer. For a graph, discuss the y-axis and x-axis and what they are indicating. Interpret data points on the graph and explain what they mean (you may at times be asked about specific points). Does anything stand out as significant based on what you observe? If you need a refresher on the different aspects of a graph, do a simple Google search for "graph interpretation" to find resources.

Ways to Rephrase:

- Enter the room and perform the following calculations...
- Convert the medication amount from milligrams to grams.

5. DISCUSS A PASTIME OUTSIDE OF SCHOOL AND HOW THE SKILLS ACQUIRED WILL HELP IN YOUR CAREER.

By now you know the admissions committee is looking for more than great experience and a solid GPA. They want interesting, well-rounded candidates who bring something unique to the upcoming class.

I've heard amazing answers in mock interviews, including sky diving, competitive ballroom dancing, cooking, traveling, and even building Legos! Some candidates are involved with unique activities, such as providing makeup classes to patients in cancer treatment. If those examples make you feel like you have nothing to share, stop. You do! Where do you find your enjoyment? Not everyone is jumping out of planes, but you most likely have interests besides medicine.

My response: I have always loved crafting. Whether learning a new skill, trying out painting, or attempting knitting, I love using my hands to create new things. My family is artistic, so I've had access to arts and crafts supplies to experiment with. In college, I opened an Etsy shop selling handmade hair accessories as a fundraiser for mission trips to Jamaica and Amsterdam. As I've matured, my crafting has shifted into DIY around the house and painting furniture.

Learning these skills has allowed me to adapt by using creativity to solve problems. I'll follow tutorials or videos, but sometimes I have to determine an alternative way to complete a task with what I have available. Besides providing stress relief during PA school, through crafting, my ability to problem solve has improved and will make me a better PA. I know I'll face issues, whether it's trying to get the right medication for a patient or having difficult patients, but my ability to think outside of the box will be beneficial in these situations. I've already utilized these skills in my job as a CNA when adjusting schedules if a patient requires more immediate attention while I still must get other jobs done. I've learned efficiency by taking things step-by-step, the same way I would complete a craft project.

(Do you see how much I fit in there? I gave personal details about my family, discussed my mission trips, shared an interest, let them know I worked as a CNA, and showed I've thought about how my experiences would help me in the future.)

Ways to rephrase:

- If you could have any other job, besides being a PA or working in the medical field, what would you do?
- Discuss an experience that allowed you to learn something important about yourself.

- What do you enjoy outside of work and school?

6. YOU ARE ON THE COMMITTEE TO HIRE A NEW FACULTY MEMBER FOR THE PA PROGRAM. WHAT CHARACTERISTICS AND/OR QUALITIES WOULD YOU LOOK FOR WHEN SELECTING AN EFFECTIVE TEACHER?

This question is basically asking for the strengths you find most important in a person, and more specifically, a PA and a teacher. What can your future program's faculty do to help you succeed?

A few desirable qualities include kindness, approachability, and a strong work ethic. I like a teacher who is willing to listen and wants me to receive the best education. PA school faculty have been in your position and know it can get tough at times, allowing them to empathize and offer support when necessary. I would also look for extensive experience, which would benefit students.

Reflect on your most effective teachers from undergrad to demonstrate what you would appreciated and what you would prefer to change. Why did you enjoy these teacher's courses? The professors I remember from undergrad were energetic and enthusiastic about the subjects they were teaching, which made me excited too.

An MMI interview is not likely to directly ask why you applied to their program, but a question like this is an opportunity to discuss what attracted you. Show you have done your research on the program and the current faculty, as well as what they currently have in place to help students. Look at the faculty to student ratio and whether they have small groups or dedicated advisors in place.

Ways to Rephrase:

- What are the 3 most important aspects in evaluating a PA program? What about a PA student?

- What can our faculty do for you?
- What accommodations will you need to successfully complete this program?

7. IF YOU COULD DO ANYTHING ELSE AND KNOW YOU WOULD BE SUCCESSFUL, WHAT WOULD YOU DO?

This is not a trick question to see if you are truly dedicated to being a PA, but merely an attempt to learn something about you. Similar to asking about your future career goals and aspirations, you should have interests outside of medicine.

During an interview, I was asked a version of this question and my immediate response was to own a wedding dress store. Immediately after those words left my mouth, I was mortified. What kind of an answer is that? What does that say about me? Thankfully, my interviewers really enjoyed my answer because they knew I was completely honest. I tend to lose any type of filter during interviews apparently.

I went on to share how I enjoyed shopping and would love to have a boutique or business someday. Those aspirations did not diminish my desire to be a PA, but I discussed other interests and my love for TLC's "Say Yes to the Dress."

When conducting mock interviews, I frequently hear answers along the lines of being a teacher or starting a non-profit. If you would genuinely prefer that career if you weren't becoming a PA, great! If you're saying what you think your interviewer wants to hear, think again. Be honest with your answers. Some of my favorite responses have included becoming a chef or a travel blogger! These answers are interesting and I enjoy hearing about my interviewee's passions.

What NOT to Say: The only wrong answer to this question is that you would only want to be a PA. They already know you want to be a

PA, so provide additional information to help your interviewer learn more about your diverse interests.

Also avoid saying a physician, or anything else in the medical field. That's not the point of the question. They aren't asking about another position in healthcare, so avoid raising a red flag about your motivations.

8. DISCUSS A TIME YOU HAD TO RESOLVE A CONFLICT.

Everyone has encountered a conflict at some point. It's a side effect of human interaction. While technically a behavioral style question, when asked during an MMI, you'll have significantly more time to expand on the situation and your resolution.

Open questions can make people stumble and seek clarification. If the prompt does not provide specifics (work, school, healthcare setting, etc.), you have room to use your own interpretation. You should have plenty of options to choose from, and based on the exercises in Chapter 13, you should have an arsenal of appropriate experiences. Here are examples of potential conflicts:

- A disagreement with a sibling or family member
- A quarrel between friends
- A difference of opinion with a co-worker
- An issue within a group project at school

Your example doesn't need to be dramatic because it's not about what happened or who was right. I want to know how you fixed it, and what the overarching lesson was. Don't just tell your story and stop. Your interviewer doesn't just want to hear about your issue, but instead they want to see you have developed problem solving skills.

Bonus Points: Relate the lesson to how it specifically prepared you to be a better PA student or PA. Directly make that connection for your interviewer instead of assuming they understand your point. Bring your answer full circle.

Ways to Rephrase:

- Tell me about a time you worked with someone you didn't like.
- Discuss a time you had to communicate effectively under pressure.
- Talk about a time you had to disagree with someone to get a positive outcome.

9. WHAT ARE YOU FAMOUS FOR?

This question is worded in an intimidating way. Famous? Me? My first instinct is nothing at all. I won a Harry Potter costume contest in fourth grade, but I wouldn't say that makes me "famous."

Don't get caught up on the wording of the question. The objective is to uncover your strengths and learn how you are perceived by your peers. In undergrad, I was known as a planner. I helped many fellow classmates map out their schedules and choose classes to reach their goals (similar to what I do now with The PA Platform). I was organized and knew when assignments were due, what material was on the next test, and which professors to take for each course.

While my schedule planning skills never went "viral," this trait followed me to PA school. I was aware of available jobs in the area and the reputations of clinical preceptors. If you have trouble figuring out what makes you stand apart, ask friends and family to assist. It's difficult to evaluate ourselves.

Ways to Rephrase:

- What are you well known for?
- Why do people recognize you?

10. YOU ARE CARING FOR AN OBESE PATIENT ON MULTIPLE MEDICATIONS, SOME OF WHICH ARE CAUSING SIDE EFFECTS. WOULD YOU RECOMMEND A CHANGE IN MEDICATIONS OR LIFESTYLE?

This is a logic/debate question. You are given a situation to fix with your personal opinion. There's no right or wrong answer, but it is valuable to see both sides when evaluating a controversial issue. Make a choice, explain your position, and back it up. Here's a step-by-step process to "think out loud" when practicing these questions:

- Restate the prompt and explain your role in the scenario. If it's not clear in the prompt, choose the position that makes the most sense. In the above prompt it does not explicitly say whether you are a PA. You could start with, " I am assuming I am the PA caring for the patient in this scenario. I need to determine if this obese patient on multiple medications should change their lifestyle or medication because they are experiencing side effects from some medications." Show your understanding of the prompt.
- Present the pros and cons of each option. For this scenario, we have lifestyle change versus medication change. The pros of lifestyle changes include weight loss, overall increased health with a healthier diet and focus on exercise, and possibly the need for less medications, which leads to fewer side effects. On the downside, this is a difficult decision requiring patient compliance and cooperation, and it may take time for the patient to gradually transition off of any medications. The pros of changing medications are a possible decrease in

bothersome side effects, while on the flip side, the new medications could also have negative side effects.

- Once you've broken down the options, make a decision. It is fine to discuss or consider both options with the patient and offer choices, but ultimately, what would you "prefer" as asked in the prompt? There is no right answer. Personally, I would encourage lifestyle changes for a set period of time before changing medications, unless the particular side effects were debilitating or preventing the patient from making lifestyle changes. I would educate the patient on steps to improve their overall health in an attempt to discontinue some of the medications that are causing problems.

When practicing ethical questions, use these same techniques as if the question was MMI style.

11. YOU DISCOVER A CLASSMATE IS ROMANTICALLY INVOLVED WITH HER PRECEPTOR. WHAT SHOULD BE DONE, IF ANYTHING? ENTER THE ROOM AND DISCUSS YOUR POSITION.

While the "think out loud" technique applies, there's more pressure because you must decide how far you're willing to go to remedy an ethical scenario once aware.

There are plenty of reasons this is an unethical situation. Being equivalent to a student dating a teacher, even at the graduate level this is considered inappropriate. Consider the possible ramifications. The student, while losing focus on learning patient care, could be receiving special treatment, not to mention the preceptor's lack of professional judgement in crossing the line to date a student. Address reasons this is unethical, and then go into the pros and cons of your options.

This situation is analogous to knowing a fellow student is

cheating their way through PA school. The student is making a poor decision, and because you know about it, you have the responsibility to take action. Here are some options: approach the student and explain directly why you don't agree with their choice, go to an advisor or clinical coordinator to make them aware of the situation, or offer to go with the student to address this with a faculty member.

What Not to Do: Nothing. Ultimately, you should make the decision to inform the program of anything you perceive as unethical. If you know about a situation, particularly in an interview setting, it is your responsibility to do **something,** even if you feel uncomfortable or would rather not get involved. This scenario is evaluating your morals and response when faced with an ethical dilemma.

Ways to Rephrase:

- What would you do if you saw a classmate cheating on an exam?

12. A FRIEND IN YOUR CLASS CONFIDES IN YOU THAT HIS MOTHER WAS RECENTLY DIAGNOSED WITH BREAST CANCER. HE IS OVERWHELMED AND MAY DROP OUT OF SCHOOL TO SPEND TIME WITH HIS MOTHER. HOW DO YOU COUNSEL YOUR FRIEND?

Empathy is the goal. Can you relate to a fellow student and help him/her through a tough situation? What advice and assistance would you offer? Are you a good friend? What kind of classmate will you be?

While you want to encourage your classmate to continue in the program, it's hard not to realize how this student may feel compelled to support his mom. Talk through the pros and cons of each decision with your fellow student.

Here are dialogue examples, but go with your gut:

- If you need to talk about it, I'm here for you.
- I would be happy to go to your advisor and see if options are available so you can be there for your mom and continue the program.
- If you need help studying or taking notes, I'm available for you, as well as our other classmates.
- Have you talked to your mom about what she thinks you should do? You've worked so hard, and your mom may want to see you complete your goals.
- Whatever you decide, I'll stand by you, but I am willing to help in whatever way possible that will help you complete the program.

You should be reassuring and encouraging. From your response, your interviewer will determine how you would personally respond if faced with a similar situation. Would you stick it out and try to complete PA school or leave to be with your family? This is a tough decision with no right or wrong answer.

Bonus Points: If you've had a personal experience similar to the one presented, share if you feel comfortable. Using your background helps relate to patients and colleagues, and makes your advice more credible.

13. YOU ARE A DERMATOLOGY PA. A PATIENT STATES THEY ARE OUT OF OPIOID PAIN MEDICATION AND UNABLE TO GET MORE FROM THEIR PAIN MANAGEMENT PHYSICIAN FOR ANOTHER FEW WEEKS. WHAT DO YOU DO?

The opioid crisis is a current hot topic in the American healthcare system. It's an epidemic and anyone working in medicine has to be aware of the impact they could have. Working in dermatology I don't typically write pain medications, but patients ask for refills, and it can be uncomfortable. Here's what this scenario is looking for:

- Are you aware of current issues in healthcare?
- Can you have confidence in your decisions as a PA?
- What value do you put on the relationship between a PA and the supervising physician?
- Are you willing to make a decision that may upset a patient?

Even without medical knowledge of how opioid medications work, indications, or regulations, you can sufficiently respond to this prompt. Use creativity to think of alternatives to offer the patient to protect them and yourself: a different non-opioid pain medication, an attempt to contact their pain management doctor to inquire about cancellations, or reassurance that this decision is in their best interest.

This type of situation could warrant a conversation with your supervising physician to ensure you're on the same page. Another consideration is circumstances as to why the patient is taking the pain medication, and if it is not dermatology related, it's out of your scope of practice to write this prescription in any scenario. Ultimately, if it is inappropriate to give a patient a medication, you shouldn't be pressured. Your interviewers are looking for confident candidates who will become confident PAs.

14. YOU ARE SEEING A PATIENT WHO IS A GYMNAST AND CURRENTLY TRAINING FOR THE OLYMPICS. THE PATIENT'S MOTHER IS UPSET BECAUSE THE PATIENT RECENTLY GAINED 3 POUNDS. ENTER THE ROOM AND ADDRESS THIS SITUATION.

During an MMI, you may be asked to role-play. Any ethical scenario can easily be turned into this type of situation with students, faculty, or volunteers acting out roles of the patient, parent, friend, etc. This is difficult to practice. If you have hands-on patient experience, you shouldn't have trouble roleplaying because the purpose is evaluating your interactions with people and if you're able to communicate well.

For this scenario specifically, you have to tiptoe around the sensitive subject of a parent asking you to encourage something unhealthy for their child. This does not require medical knowledge. You must keep your calm (even if the mom gets angry) and advocate for what you think is best for the patient. The observers are looking for you to diffuse the situation in a level-headed manner. This is where your experience with patients comes into play. Use the skills you've learned from interacting with people. Even though the situation is "fake," approach it as if you are working in a real clinic and try to get into character.

What NOT To Do: Become defensive or aggressive, even if you're feeling attacked. Stay calm and hold your ground. No one wants a hot head in their program.

15. A BOAT IS SINKING. THERE IS A LIFEBOAT FOR ONE PERSON. THE PASSENGERS INCLUDE A 75-YEAR-OLD PHYSICIAN, 50-YEAR-OLD ARMY OFFICER, 24-YEAR-OLD TEACHER, AND A 6-YEAR OLD. WHO GETS THE SPOT?

This is my favorite example of a question without an answer. How are you supposed to pick one of these individuals? You could never be right or wrong. What's your first instinct?

As we've discussed, in a situation with multiple options, weigh the pros and cons. When I ask this question in mock interviews, most people immediately choose the 6-year-old. I find this interesting because once you dig deeper, you may feel differently. Either way, it's a personal decision. Let's break down each option:

- *75-year-old physician* - A physician may be most equipped to care for any sick or injured passengers, but that knowledge may enable them to survive if they ran into trouble on the lifeboat. As the oldest option, is it fair to say they have lived the most life and should sacrifice their position on the lifeboat?
- *50-year-old army officer* - This person would arguably have the most survival training, and potentially be most qualified to make it to shore and try to get assistance for the sinking boat. Those same principles could be argued for why the officer should stay and help remaining members survive.
- *24-year-old teacher-* As a young person, a teacher has potential because they teach the next physicians and army officers, so could they have the biggest impact if they survive? Would they have the necessary skills to make it though?
- *6-year-old* - It's easy to assume the child should get first dibs on the lifeboat as the youngest member with the most life left to live. To play the devil's advocate, do you

truly think a 6-year-old could navigate a small lifeboat to dry land independently? Would fear or lack of strength get in the way? In my mind, that would be a tough call.

Personally, I have some questions I would like answered before making my decision, although that information may not be provided. How far is the lifeboat from the shore? Is help on the way? Does anyone know the boat is sinking? Can I choose the two smallest people and put both on the lifeboat? You can demonstrate your thought process by discussing each option available before making your final decision. Ultimately, you must decide.

Bonus Points: This prompt is commonly used as a group debate activity, and instead of making a decision independently, you must decide as a group.

CHAPTER 8

GROUP INTERVIEWS

There are two types of group interviews, and we'll break down each of them: **Panel and Activity**. During any group session, the main objective is showing your ability to function as a team member and demonstrate your ability to work well with others.

There are a few reasons a program chooses to utilize group interviews. Besides seeing how you communicate with others, it allows the interviewers to directly compare candidates. While I don't want you to think of the group interview as a competition, at the end of the day, they can only choose a predetermined number of people and everyone needs to demonstrate good interpersonal skills. These types of interviews allow the school to save time and money by speaking to more than one applicant at a time.

GROUP PANEL INTERVIEW

A group panel interview is more like a traditional interview, but with multiple applicants. These can be set up differently and the amount of applicants being interviewed at one time will vary. There may be multiple interviewers as well. For example, you could have one interviewer asking three applicants questions, or three interviewers asking four applicants questions. The options are endless!

You may all be asked the same question, or different questions for each applicant. They may go down the line or ask questions in a "free-for-all" style where you volunteer to answer, but you should still have an opportunity to participate. There are benefits to being assertive and going first, but if you need time to think, it may be in your best interest to hold off on answering right away. The types of questions tend to be traditional, behavioral, or ethical interview questions such as those covered in the previous chapters.

It's important to interact with your fellow interviewees and build from their answers and experiences with your own personal insights. It would be weird if you acted like they weren't there. Try to remember names of other applicants and refer to them individually.

These types of interviews can be intimidating for a couple of reasons: the fear that someone will "steal" your answer and wanting to limit your answer to an appropriate time. Both are reasonable considerations.

There is the chance someone may say a similar response to your planned reply, but typically the questions asked have multiple answers or will come from your personal experience. In mock interviews, the example I use is:

"What is the biggest challenge facing PAs?"

The most common answer is something along the lines of patients not understanding the PA profession fully. For this example, let's say the person sitting next to you is Johnny, and he says this exact answer. Shoot! What are you supposed to do now?

Instead of getting flustered and shutting down, you've got to think on your feet. If you have a back-up answer, go with that, but if not, use the technique of building off of Johnny's answer. This is a great chance to agree with him, and demonstrate your knowledge of the subject and experience. You can say something along the lines of, "I agree with Johnny. There is a huge lack of knowledge among patients regarding the PA profession, and I've witnessed this through my work or shadowing experiences." If time allows, feel free to expand on what exactly you observed. Using examples gives your answer more credibility.

It isn't uncommon to feel intimidated by hearing the experience of others. Someone will always have a better GPA or more hours, but you have things they don't! This knowledge should give you confidence. Don't let self doubt hinder your ability to shine or feel shy discussing your strengths and experiences, even in front of other applicants.

In a group setting, you should be aware of how long your answers are. Be a bit more concise and direct than you would be during a traditional interview, and don't let your answers exceed 2 minutes at the most.

GROUP ACTIVITY

The purpose of a group activity is to observe how you work as a team member and your interactions with other applicants. A huge part of success in PA school and being a good PA is interacting well with others and supporting your colleagues. The ability to interact as a team player is vital, therefore schools are seeking individuals who already portray this skill. This can be presented as a group discussion or a problem solving task (think team building and ice breakers).

During a group activity, you want to encourage your fellow applicants, while showing your personality and ability to form personal opinions. You can take on a role as a leader through facilitating discussion, while showing your problem solving skills. Build off of others suggestions as you navigate the activity. If you don't feel comfortable being in the leader position, it's ok. Just make sure you're still contributing in some way. The task is to demonstrate your communication skills, your ability to form opinions, and complete the activity.

Make this a fun experience. You are in the same boat as your fellow applicants, and your team members may be some future classmates! Try not to consider this a competition, but more of a collaboration. Work on building some camaraderie between the applicants during your activity.

It's important to not become defensive or argumentative with group members. It's acceptable to cordially disagree, but be respectful in the process. Of course this should be obvious, but high stress situations can make us act differently than usual. There's a fine line between being a dictator and a wallflower, and you have to find it. Show you have distinct thoughts you fully support, and that you aren't easily swayed in your decision making.

Examples of group activities:

- Use this box of objects to design a machine to do XYZ.
- You have to decide who will receive a kidney transplant. One patient is a 75 year old who was just added to the list last week. The other option is a 55 year old patient who has been on the list for a year, but is an alcoholic. Who should get the kidney?
- Solve this puzzle...
- Build a bridge between these tables that can hold a pile of books.
- Read an article and discuss the medical/ethical issues presented.
- Take these photos and arrange them into two stories, tell the stories, and explain the similarities.

CHAPTER 9

ESSAYS

This chapter will be short and sweet! Some schools ask you to write an essay while at the interview. It may be one essay, or a few short answer questions, but typically it isn't too intense. Try not to stress too much! Writing a short essay should not rattle you or add to your nerves significantly. If you've done some preparation for your interview (like reading this book), and you wrote your own personal statement, you should be fine.

There are a few motives for having you write an essay. The first is to verify you as the author of your personal statement and see if the prose aligns. Your personal statement will be much more detailed than the essay you write during the interview, but it will be apparent if there's a large discrepancy in writing style. Programs are aware of companies that write entire essays for students.

Another objective is to ensure fluency in English. If English is not your first language, this is a chance to demonstrate your writing skills in English are high quality. PAs have to write medical notes, which need to be easily understood by other individuals who review the information in a patient's chart.

When writing an essay, show the ability to form an opinion. You need to be capable of organizing your thoughts on a subject in a concise way and conveying them on paper.

When it was time for my essay portion during interviews, I had a strategy in mind. I wasn't going to attempt a literary piece of art. I simply wanted to get my answer down as quickly as possible knowing there could be a limited amount of time. At my interview, we were given 30 minutes after our interview to complete the essay portion. Some interviews provide the prompt at the beginning of the day, you work on writing throughout the day, and turn it in before leaving.

I resorted to 5th grade essay writing techniques. Just the basics!

- An introduction with what I was planning to discuss
- 3 body paragraphs with their own main point and supporting details
- A short conclusion summarizing the entire essay

Nothing too crazy happening in my PA interview essays. Space may be limited, and there's only so much one can say in 1-2 pages. Keep in mind that expectations are not extravagant for this essay, and the weight of your actual face to face interview is much more influential.

The essay could be a specific topic, or just be a traditional interview question, like "Why do you want to be a PA?" It could also be an ethical question. You may be asked to read an article and discuss your opinions about the medical or ethical issue presented. Be prepared for any of those off the wall questions too, such as "If you could have any super power, what would it be and why?" Prior to your interview, practice writing out a 1-page response to any of the questions in this book.

CHAPTER 10

QUESTIONS TO ASK YOUR INTERVIEWER

Throughout mock interviews, one of the most common questions asked before we wrap up is:

What should I ask them?

Valid question. When faced with "Well, do you have any questions for us?" I completely understand not wanting to sit there like a deer in the headlights. This is your one opportunity to get additional information and show your interest, as well as your last impression with the interviewer.

Consider two approaches - school focused or personal. Don't ask about anything already covered in a tour, on the website, or by students as this looks like you weren't paying attention. Keep questions open ended instead of yes/no and avoid asking questions that portray you as skeptical of the school or your abilities to succeed.

Here are some examples of questions NOT to ask:

- Why should I pick your program over a different one?
- What do you do for students if they are failing?
- Why is your PANCE rate lower?
- Why did less students take the PANCE than matriculated?
- Why didn't three students graduate?

While these are valid concerns, it might be better to inquire on a private forum or from students rather than during your actual interview. You don't want the program to feel you are less than excited about being in their class. Attempt to keep questions positive and relative to why you need to be in their class.

Besides school-specific questions, you can ask personal questions of your interviewers as well. While they are getting to know you, this is your chance to also get to know them. If they ask an interesting question, feel free to ask them the same one! I used that tactic and my interviewers enjoyed being asked something out of the ordinary.

Here are some examples of questions you may want to ask:

- Where did you go to PA school?
- What made you choose your specialty?
- What do students do for fun?
- What is your favorite part of teaching anatomy, pharmacology, etc?
- Why did you choose to teach PA school?
- What can applicants do to make themselves stand out for your school?
- What qualities do you look for in PA students?

PART 3

FOLLOW-UP

CHAPTER 11

AFTER THE INTERVIEW

First of all, take a deep breath. You survived! Let's address the logistics of steps you can take while playing the waiting game.

WHAT SHOULD YOU DO AFTER THE INTERVIEW?

A common question in regards to appropriate etiquette following the interview is, "What do I do now? Should I send thank you notes? An email? Who should I send them to? Will it look bad if I don't send them?"

Post-interview etiquette is debatable, but it is reasonable to send a follow up if you had a good interview experience and would like to extend gratitude for the opportunity. I don't necessarily think you should feel required to send thank you notes. They likely do not make a difference in a committee's decision on acceptance, and are more of a formality and courtesy than anything else.

No matter how you look at it, it's always nice to get a handwritten note. If you are wanting to send something to the program to say thank you, sending a written card in the mail is a great option. If that's not your cup of tea, it's alright because we live in an era where email has become the norm. An email is a quicker option to express your thanks. I've heard of people putting a letter in the mail and then getting a rejection the same day. Whoops! A rejection shouldn't affect your decision to be gratuitous though. If you plan on sending a note of thanks, it doesn't matter which method you choose, so proceed based on your comfort level.

Knowing where to send your note or email can be a hurdle. Attempt to obtain this information at your interview. Oftentimes, it's provided on a handout or given directly by the program coordinator. If you forget (probably due to nerves, which is completely reasonable), contact the program coordinator or look on the program website after the interview, and ascertain if either resource can provide the mailing address or emails you need. If you don't recall your interviewer's name(s), you may be out of luck with getting this information at a later date, however you can in the least send a general letter to the director.

Keep your note short and sweet because you want to be respectful of your recipient's time. Thank your interviewer for their time and for the opportunity to learn more about their program. If there's anything memorable or specific you discussed during your time with the interviewer, refer to that in your note to add a personal touch.

While thank you notes are a nice gesture, don't let them stress you out. At the end of the day, it's a courtesy, and not a deal breaker that will impact your acceptance to PA school. Don't let the idea of collecting names and addresses plus writing thank you notes cause anxiety. If it's too much to handle right now, that's ok! To be perfectly honest, I did not send thank you notes. During interviews, I was in the middle of finals and actually had to reschedule some tests, which was my priority at the time. Nevertheless, I was still accepted!

BE PATIENT

Next, be patient. Easier said than done, right? Resist the temptation to contact the program immediately to find out if a decision has been made. Annoying the program will not benefit you, and if anything, may affect you negatively. Even though it's difficult, have faith in the process.

REFLECT

You never know when you will receive another interview invitation, but don't wait to use the experience you just had to improve your skills for future interviews. Think back on the questions asked and your responses. If you're like me, you may have blacked out during some of those making it difficult to recall exactly what was said. That's okay.

Think about questions that stumped you and ones that got you a little flustered. Try to dissect why these questions were tough. Do you need to do more research? Should you review your application before the next interview? Do you need to study the mission statement? Did you do a good job of using examples and bringing your answers full circle?

You'll always walk out of the room feeling you could have done better or said things differently. Don't beat yourself up! Take that experience and use it to improve for the next interview. No matter how much you prepare, you'll still find room for improvement. Just move on and be prepared to do it again if needed. (Fingers crossed you won't need to though!)

WHEN TO FOLLOW UP

After a reasonable period of time, which is program dependent, if you've heard nothing, consider contacting the program to see if they made a decision. Occasionally, letters get lost in the mail, and you don't want a fluke to be the reason you don't have a seat. A fellow classmate received no feedback for a few months and called the school. Turns out her letter was sent weeks before and the following day was her last chance to get a deposit in!

A good way to monitor whether schools are sending out acceptances is with www.physicianassistantforum.com. They have specific school threads, and fellow applicants share whether they are hearing back from interviews. Facebook groups, like The Pre-PA Club, are also good sources to follow during interview season. If it appears a school is sending out acceptances, I would recommend giving it 2-4 weeks. If you haven't heard at that point, contact the program coordinator or admissions director to inquire if they have made a decision regarding your acceptance status. Don't be surprised if you get a generic response, which means, yes, more waiting.

CHAPTER 12

FAQ

At this point, we've covered a lot of information, but you may have additional questions that need to be addressed. I'll cover those here, but feel free to email or DM on Instagram additional questions if you don't find the answers you're looking for. You can also join The Pre-PA Club Group on Facebook and post questions as myself and the other coaches at The PA Platform frequently chime in.

WHEN WILL I GET MY INTERVIEW INVITES?

They can roll out at any time, so be prepared. Sometimes you won't get much warning. Following www.physicianassistantforum.com is a good resource to see when others are getting invitations, and to keep up with the status of a school's interview season.

HOW WILL I GET I GET MY INTERVIEW INVITES?

This depends on the school, but you should find this information on the PA forums as well. It can come in any form- email (most common), phone call, or letter. Make sure to check your junk email folder regularly. Bottom line, even if you haven't received notification, be ready to go at any time!

WHY AM I NOT GETTING MORE INTERVIEWS?

Schools tend to have specific aspects they are looking for, and hopefully you have what it takes. Try not to be discouraged if you aren't hearing back as quickly as you would like. Keep an eye on the forums to see if schools you applied to have even sent out invitations.

Consider looking back at your application to reflect on why you aren't getting call backs or why you've had rejections. In addition, double check that you meet minimum requirements for the programs you applied to. Review your experience details on CASPA and personal statement to evaluate whether you were personal enough and if you covered the most essential information.

Towards the end of the cycle, if you didn't get the results you were hoping for, follow up with the programs you applied to. Some programs are willing to provide feedback on where you need to improve and what separated you from applicants who were interviewed and ultimately accepted.

I HAVE A CONFLICT. CAN I CHANGE MY INTERVIEW DATE?

Yikes! This is a tough one because generally the answer is no. It sounds harsh, but schools have an abundance of qualified applicants to fill your spot, and scheduling needs to be precise. Should the need arise, it doesn't hurt to ask about rescheduling, but be prepared to assess your priorities and make a decision.

WHAT SHOULD I BRING TO THE INTERVIEW?

Technically, you don't need to bring anything that isn't specifically asked for by the program. Since CASPA is all online, if part of your application is missing, the program can pull it up.

For my interviews, I carried a small purse. It contained my phone (which was off for the entire interview), a pen, small notepad, and my keys. I kept a copy of my application and resume in my car just in case it was requested. Some applicants bring a padfolio with their documents, which is fine if it calms your nerves to have the information with you or keeps your hands occupied.

Here are some additional items to could consider bringing:

- Parking pass
- Directions
- Updated transcripts showing new final grades
- A copy of your resume
- A headshot
- Additional letters of recommendation
- Anything else you want added to your file

CAN I REFER TO MY NOTES OR USE MY PADFOLIO DURING MY INTERVIEW?

No. You should be completely engaged with your interviewer(s) during the actual interview portion and not distracted by notes. This would be seen as slightly strange and definitely unprofessional.

WHAT SHOULD I DO WITH MY LUGGAGE DURING THE INTERVIEW?

You have options - inquire if the hotel can hold it or ask, in advance, if you can store it at the school during your interview. If you have a quick flight afterwards, it may not be convenient to get back to the hotel and pick it up. A rental car is another consideration so you could keep your belongings there for convenience.

DO I NEED TO SHAVE MY BEARD FOR INTERVIEWS?

Beards are pretty common these days and there's a big difference in a well-trimmed, nicely groomed beard and a Duck Dynasty style, mountain man beard. Facial hair is acceptable as long as you look professional, but if it makes you self conscious, go for the clean shaven look.

HOW WILL THEY FEEL ABOUT PIERCINGS AND TATTOOS?

Piercings are fine within reason. If you have multiple visible face or ear piercings, removing these or wearing something extremely subtle would be the best option. Tattoos should be covered on interview day. Most schools have policies about tattoos that basically say it's fine to have them as long as they can't be seen. This is changing a little bit in the workplace, but err on the side of trying to look as professional as possible!

IS IT OKAY FOR ME TO TALK ABOUT MY RELIGION OR FAITH?

My rule of thumb: if something is an important part of your life, you should feel comfortable discussing it in your interview. Faith and religion tend to fall into this category. Personally, I spoke about my involvement in church during my interview because most of my volunteer and missions experience was through my campus ministry during college. It would have felt strange to not include those things in my interview, especially since they were on my application.

I BOMBED MY INTERVIEW. WHAT SHOULD I DO?

Stop beating yourself up and start thinking about why you did poorly. And did you really do that bad? You'll always feel there's something you could have done better no matter how much you prepare. The important thing at this point is to figure out what you need to work on to improve for the next interview.

HOW WILL THEY NOTIFY ME OF ACCEPTANCE?

This will depend on the program. You may find some info on the forums, but it could range from email to letter to call, and rarely an in person acceptance on the day of your interview!

I WAS ACCEPTED TO ONE SCHOOL AND THEY WANT A DEPOSIT, BUT I'M WAITING TO HEAR BACK FROM ANOTHER PROGRAM. WHAT SHOULD I DO?

When you get an acceptance, usually you're given a short time period to make a decision. While it can be a chunk of change to secure your spot with a deposit (up to $2,000), in the long run, it's worth it to know you are in. Think very carefully about rejecting an acceptance because another position is not guaranteed.

Even if you make a deposit, it is not binding. The deposit is just to secure your spot, but you can always decline (without a refund) if you do get another acceptance.

I WAS ACCEPTED. WILL THE SCHOOL LET ME DEFER MY ACCEPTANCE FOR A YEAR?

Typically no. Similar to changing your interview date, there's always someone else who would be more than happy to take your spot. The only deferments I've heard of being granted are for legitimate medical reasons. Examples would be pregnancy or cancer treatments. If you're wanting time off to travel or save money, that's not going to fly. Think hard about giving up your seat because you'll have to go through the entire process again and a second acceptance is not guaranteed.

CHAPTER 13

INTERVIEW PREPARATION WORKSHEETS

Make a list of everything you want the interviewer/admissions committee to know about you before you leave - personality traits, values, qualities, skills, experiences, goals, etc.

- _____
- _____
- _____

Are there any specific skills or knowledge you have that will make you a valuable member of the class?

- Are you bilingual?_____
- Can you do venipuncture, IVs, give injections, any skills that could help your classmates, etc? _____
- Is there any area that you have more expertise due to your healthcare experience, which will help you during that section in school, and you will also be able to help your classmates with (ex - worked as an MA in orthopedics/dermatology/etc)? _____

- Anything else you can think of:
  - _____
  - _____
  - _____

3 things you saw while shadowing- What did you learn? What encounters did you see the PA have with patients, co-workers, or their supervising physician? Did you see anything you want to emulate as a PA or anything you want to avoid? How did your time shadowing help you understand the role of a PA better?

  - _____
  - _____
  - _____

3 patients who made an impact on you - Did you learn something significant about being a PA or about yourself? A difficult patient? Someone you were able to help? An encounter that you had to learn from a mistake?

  - _____
  - _____
  - _____

Is there anything "questionable" on your application that you may be asked specifically about (low grades/GPA/GRE, with-drawals, lack of healthcare experience or shadowing hours)? To take it one step further, what did you learn from these situations?

  - _____
  - Improvement?_____
  - _____
  - Improvement?_____

What are 3 things <u>not on your application</u> that you want to share before you leave your interview?

- _____
- _____
- _____

So, what's next? Time to practice! Head to the next chapter to try out your interview skills with the Mock Interview Guide. If you would prefer to print a copy of these worksheets, go to http://www.thepaplatform.com/freeguide for a free download.

CHAPTER 14

MOCK INTERVIEW GUIDE

INSTRUCTIONS FOR THE APPLICANT

- If you would prefer to print a copy of the Mock Interview Guide, go to http://www.thepaplatform.com/freeguide to download a PDF.
- To simulate a realistic interview experience, you may choose to dress in what you plan to wear on interview day
- Find a quiet place where you will be comfortable and undisturbed for at least 30 minutes
- Don't look at the questions before your session so you get a more realistic experience
- Choosing how to conduct the mock interview – You may go through all of the questions in one sitting and then do feedback (recommended), or do half of the questions and stop for feedback before doing the second half.
- If a question throws you off, try to not get flustered and just move on to a different question.
- Record the session on video so you can review it

afterwards and see if you have any distracting habits. We all hate to see ourselves on camera, but you may find that you are not articulating the way you would like.

- After the session, take time with your "Interviewer" to go back through the questions and talk through your responses to identify strengths and weaknesses.
- Is there anywhere that you can use more specific examples or stories to answer the questions?
- Were there any questions you didn't feel confident about?
- Are there any stories or examples that could be used to answer multiple questions?

INSTRUCTIONS FOR THE INTERVIEWER

- Plan to spend at least 30 minutes asking questions.
- If possible, review the applicant's transcript or application beforehand. Try to make the questions more specific if possible. Look for discrepancies on the transcript, such as lower grades or lack of experience.
- Ask the questions in order, and give the applicant significant time to answer. Some questions will have qualifying statements of specifics to look for, or clarification of what the question is asking. Review the questions before starting the Mock Interview.
- Try to maintain a blank face and do not give significant feedback during the Mock Interview session.
- Ask relevant follow-up questions for elaboration.
- Try to make the interview as conversational as possible.
- Specifically pay attention to whether the applicant has distracting habits (hand movements, touching hair, repetitive phrases) or redundant answers
- Do the answers relate to why the applicant wants to be a PA, and how they will be a good PA?

- Does the applicant stop answering when appropriate and not repeat answers multiple times?
- Do you truly get the impression that the applicant wants to be a PA?
- Fill out the assessment after the session
- Go back through the questions with the applicant and discuss their answers.

QUESTIONS

Tell me a little bit about yourself.

- If applicant goes straight into why they want to be a PA, follow up with "**Tell me something about yourself that's not on your application.**"
- Did the applicant discuss themselves as a person instead of just talking about why they want to be a PA (hobbies, family, etc.)?

Why do you want to be a PA?

Did you consider any other medical professions?

- If applicant mentions learning on the medical model versus the nursing model, ask them to clarify.

How have you prepared to be a successful PA?

- Did you learn something about the applicant's skills or knowledge that makes them more qualified?

Why are you a good fit for *INSERT SCHOOL NAME*?

- Does the applicant discuss the pros of the program, as well as what they can contribute?

Have you applied elsewhere?

- Does the applicant reinforce that they want to attend the school they are currently "interviewing" at?

Tell me about your support system.

- Did you feel confident that there's nothing that would prevent the applicant from finishing the program?

What are your plans if not accepted to a PA program this year?

- Does the applicant have a practical plan that shows improvement and dedication to becoming a PA?

What is the biggest challenge facing PAs?

- Did applicant address an issue specific to PAs and not just something that is general to healthcare?

What is your biggest weakness?

- Did applicant show how they have improved on this weakness or are currently trying to improve?

Discuss a time that you have struggled academically.

- Did applicant address study skills in a way that made you feel they would be successful in PA school?

Describe some of your shadowing experience.

- Did applicant show a good understanding of the PA profession based on what they've seen while shadowing?

Where do you see yourself in 5 years?

- Did the applicant discuss long term goals, how they will give back to the PA profession and the underserved, and personal goals?

Tell me about a situation you had with a difficult patient.

Tell me about a time you had to overcome adversity.

Discuss a time you had to make an ethical decision.

Describe a high stress situation you've been in and how you handled it.

If you were a PA, how would you feel if a patient didn't want to see you?

- Did the applicant attempt to educate the patient, but also respect their wishes?

How would you describe the role of a PA to a patient?

- Answer should include - evaluating patients, making diagnoses, developing treatments, ordering and interpreting tests, prescribing medication under the supervision of a physician

Your supervising physician asks you to give a medication to a patient, but you are concerned it could be harmful. How do you handle this situation?

- Did the applicant portray autonomy in making decisions?

Discuss a time that you have resolved a conflict.

MOCK INTERVIEW ASSESSMENT

Assign points from 1-5 based on each category, and then use the total to get an overall feel of how the interview went.

COMMUNICATION

- Clearly articulated thoughts ___
- Used specific examples ___
- Answers were appropriate length ___
- No slang or distracting words/phrases ___
- Correct grammar ___
- Answers were genuine (not rehearsed or robotic) ___
- Conveyed information not on application or resume ___
- Discussed personal traits ___
- Conveyed why applicant would be a successful PA ___

TOTAL: /45 Total Possible Points

PRESENCE

- Professional appearance (if applicable) ___
- Good eye contact ___
- Appropriate tone/volume of voice ___
- Free from fidgeting/ nervous habits ___
- Maintained composure even if challenged ___

TOTAL: /25 Total Possible Points

SELF-CONFIDENCE/ATTITUDE

- Appeared at ease ___
- Showed enthusiasm ___
- Appropriate level of confidence ___
- Pleasant disposition ___
- Responded assertively to questions ___
- Portrayed passion for the PA profession ___

TOTAL: /30 Total Possible Points
OVERALL TOTAL: /100 points

While this scoring is slightly arbitrary (and depending on who's working with you, they may feel inclined to give you a perfect score regardless), it should provide direction as far as what areas need improvement and what you should be working on to improve your overall impression at an interview.

COMMENTS:

- Any bad habits? ("um," "like," other repetitive phrases, touching hair or glasses)
- Did applicant stop answering questions when appropriate? (As opposed to repeating the answer they already used.)
- Assuming you didn't already know the applicant, did you feel like you got to know them as a person besides their application/resume after the interview?
- Did you truly feel that the applicant has a passion for becoming a PA?

CHAPTER 15

MASTER QUESTION LIST

1. Tell me a little bit about yourself.
2. What do you like to do for fun?
3. Tell me about some of your hobbies.
4. What is the last book you read?
5. What is your life saying?
6. Tell me what your typical day looks like.
7. Introduce yourself.
8. What makes you unique?
9. Discuss a pastime you enjoy.
10. Why do you want to be a PA?
11. What made you interested in medicine?
12. How did you find out about the PA profession?
13. What stood out to you about the profession?
14. Why do you want to be a PA for the rest of your working career?
15. Are you passionate about this profession?
16. What have you done to prepare for PA school and your future career as a PA?
17. Have you considered medical school?

18. Did you ever want to be a physical therapist?
19. Why don't you want to be a doctor?
20. What influenced your decision to become a PA?
21. Tell me about your motivations for becoming a PA.
22. Why have you chosen to pursue the PA profession?
23. How did you become interested in becoming a PA?
24. What part of becoming a PA and practicing medicine as a PA are you looking forward to the most?
25. Why do you want to attend this program?
26. What makes you unique?
27. What makes you a good candidate for our program?
28. What can you bring to the class?
29. How would the class benefit as a whole from having you as a member?
30. What makes you diverse?
31. What would our class be missing if we didn't pick you?
32. Why should we pick you?
33. What sets you apart?
34. What is appealing about the location of (program name)?
35. What qualities or skills do you have that would make you a valuable student and classmate?
36. Why did you decide to choose a program that's out of state?
37. Why did you apply to a program that's close to/far away from your hometown?
38. Are you aware of what a PA does?
39. Explain the role of a PA to a patient.
40. Describe what a PA does.
41. What have you observed while shadowing?
42. What have you seen that has influenced your decision to become a PA?
43. Do you fully understand the role of a PA?
44. Pretend you are asked to speak to a group of high school students and explain the PA profession.

45. What makes you an ideal applicant for PA school?
46. What do you see as the future of PAs?
47. How do you see the role of PAs changing in the future?
48. What have you done to prepare for PA school?
49. How have you prepared to be a successful PA?
50. What specific skills do you have that will benefit you or your classmates during PA school?
51. What experience in your background will make you a good PA?
52. When did you decide to pursue PA school?
53. How were you initially introduced to the PA profession?
54. How did you discover the PA profession?
55. When did you find out about the PA profession?
56. What have you done to increase your chances of being accepted to a PA program?
57. What experiences have you had that will influence how you practice as a PA?
58. What is your biggest weakness?
59. What is your biggest personality flaw?
60. What would your co-workers say is your greatest weakness?
61. What is one thing your classmates dislike about you?
62. If you are not accepted into this program, what do you think would be the reason?
63. What is your biggest strength?
64. What makes you stand out compared to other candidates?
65. What is the best thing about your personality?
66. What would your last employer say about you?
67. Why should we choose you?
68. Have you applied elsewhere?
69. If you applied elsewhere, how did you choose those programs?

70. What would make you choose another program over this one?
71. Where else have you applied?
72. Have you interviewed anywhere else?
73. Who is the most important member on a healthcare team?
74. How does a PA fit into the healthcare team?
75. What is a dependent practitioner, and how do you feel about practicing as one?
76. If you had to be a member of the healthcare team other than a PA, what would you choose?
77. Discuss the relationship between a PA and a nurse.
78. What is the biggest challenge facing PAs?
79. What will be most difficult for you as a practicing PA?
80. How do you feel PAs are limited?
81. What are difficulties PAs are facing?
82. What are the negative aspects of being a PA?
83. What are some of the most significant issues PAs currently face and will have to face in the future?
84. If you could change one thing about the PA profession, what would you change?
85. What do you expect a typical week in PA school to look like?
86. What do you expect of a typical day in PA school?
87. Why do you think you would be successful in PA school?
88. Assure us you will do well in PA school and not drop out.
89. What study skills do you have?
90. How do you stay organized?
91. Have you been able to speak with current students?
92. How many hours a week do you plan on studying while in PA school?
93. What kind of barriers, besides financial, do you see involved with being a PA student?

94. What have you done, besides shadowing, to prepare for PA school?

95. How has your background prepared you for the intense physical and mental rigor it takes to become a PA?

96. In your opinion, what will be your greatest challenge in completing PA school?

97. Reassure me you will not fail out of the program.

98. Is there anything that you foresee preventing you from completing the program?

99. How do you study best?

100. Tell me about a time you struggled academically.

101. Do you study best individually or in a group?

102. Do you work better as an individual or with a team?

103. How would you describe your overall academic performance?

104. What will be your hardest class if accepted?

105. How are you academically prepared for PA school?

106. How do you handle blood and gore?

107. Have you ever seen someone die?

108. Do you have a weak stomach?

109. How would having a family/children affect your performance in PA school?

110. How will being a younger/older applicant affect your performance in the program?

111. What advantages or disadvantages would you have as a younger/older applicant?

112. Do you feel comfortable with technology?

113. Tell me about your support system.

114. Who is going to support you through school?

115. Is your family supportive of your goal to become a PA?

116. Who has encouraged you to become a PA?

117. How would you get to school?

118. Where would you live while in PA school?

119. How are your time management skills?

120. Are you able to handle multiple assignments at once?
121. Are you able to handle a busy schedule?
122. Tell me about a time you've had to multitask.
123. Did you work while getting your prerequisites?
124. What was the most challenging course of your undergraduate studies, and why?
125. What has been the highlight of your undergraduate years?
126. What extracurricular activity will benefit you most as a PA?
127. What was your biggest accomplishment from undergrad?
128. Can you explain your lower grade/low GRE/lack of shadowing or HCE?
129. Are there any discrepancies on your application you would like to discuss?
130. There's one spot left and it's between you and another candidate. The other candidate has a higher GPA. Who should be chosen?
131. What are you looking for in a PA program?
132. Why do you want to go to this specific program?
133. What does our program have to offer you?
134. What do you have to offer our program?
135. Why did you apply here?
136. Why would you choose our program instead of another program?
137. What do you find appealing about (program name)?
138. Why did you choose our program over the others?
139. What are your plans if not accepted to a PA program this year?
140. How do you plan on improving yourself if not accepted into PA school?
141. What would you do if you were not selected for this program?

142. What is the difference in the nursing model and medical model?
143. Did you consider becoming a nurse practitioner (NP)?
144. What qualities make a successful physician assistant?
145. How do you plan to practice as a PA?
146. If you were interviewing a potential PA student, what would you look for?
147. If you were chosen to hire a PA, what qualities should they have?
148. Tell me about the last physician you worked for.
149. Describe your volunteer experience.
150. What extracurricular activity will benefit you most as a PA?
151. What extracurricular activity will help you be successful in PA school?
152. Describe a leadership role you have held.
153. Do you plan on continuing to volunteer while in PA school or as a PA?
154. Is there a specific specialty or ideal job you envision for yourself as a PA?
155. Where do you see yourself in 5 years?
156. Where do you see yourself in 10 years?
157. Is there a particular field that appeals to you?
158. What are your goals in medicine?
159. How do you plan to contribute as a PA professional when finished with the program?
160. Why do you want to do primary care (or other specialty)?
161. Why do you want to help underserved populations?
162. Where do you want to work?
163. How will politics influence PAs?
164. How do you feel Trumpcare will affect PAs?
165. How do you feel the new health bill will impact healthcare?
166. Tell us about healthcare reform.

167. Do you think healthcare reform will be positive or negative for PAs? Why?

168. Do you think HMOs and PPOs are good or bad for the PA profession?

169. What are the trends of healthcare in the United States?

170. Would you feel limited by any of the state or national regulations on PAs?

171. Tell me what you know about laws for PAs in this state.

172. What law do you think limits PAs the most?

173. Are there laws you feel limit the PA profession unfairly?

174. Are there laws you feel should be passed to further the progression of the PA profession?

175. If you could change any law pertaining to the PA profession, what would you change, and why?

176. Are you familiar with any national or state level regulations for PAs?

177. Are you aware of recent changes in legislation regarding what PAs can and cannot do?

178. What are your thoughts on the newer online PA programs?

179. What are your thoughts on the new bridge programs from PA to MD/DO?

180. Are you using PA school as a stepping stone to become an MD/DO?

181. Should PA education be standardized?

182. What are your thoughts on the name "physician assistant," and the push to change to "physician associate?"

183. What do you know about the history of the PA profession.

184. What is the most selfless thing you have ever done?

185. What is the biggest responsibility you have ever been tasked with?

186. Describe a time you had to overcome adversity.

187. What is the biggest challenge you've ever faced?

188. Tell me about a time you've been judged unfairly.

189. Discuss a time you were unable to meet someone's expectations.

190. What is the most difficult thing you've ever done?

191. What is your biggest regret?

192. What one thing would you change about your undergraduate experience?

193. Why did you choose your undergraduate major? Are you happy with your choice?

194. What is one thing you would like to change about yourself?

195. Describe a disappointing moment from your life.

196. Tell me about a time you disappointed someone.

197. Have you ever been disappointed?

198. Tell me about a time you didn't meet expectations.

199. What's your worst experience?

200. If a student fails a test, is it the student's fault or the teacher's fault?

201. Tell me about a time you received negative feedback and how you used it to improve yourself.

202. Discuss a time that you received constructive criticism and how you responded.

203. Describe a time you have struggled academically, and how you dealt with it.

204. What was your most difficult class in undergrad?

205. What is the hardest class you've ever taken?

206. What non-science undergraduate course will benefit you most in PA school?

207. How would you describe your overall academic performance?

208. You are a PA. You are at a baseball game and the woman in front of you has a suspicious mole you suspect could be melanoma. What do you do?

209. You are a PA. A patient on your schedule insists on seeing an MD. How do you handle it?

210. How would you feel if a patient refused to see you because you're a PA?

211. How can you earn respect as a PA?

212. A patient is not proficient in English, and you are unfamiliar with their language. How can you assist?

213. What is something difficult you have had to discuss with someone?

214. Have you ever had to share bad news?

215. Describe a situation you have had with a difficult patient.

216. Discuss a situation with a patient that had a significant impact on you.

217. How do you deal with high stress situations? Give an example.

218. How do you handle stress?

219. Have you ever been stressed out?

220. Discuss a high stress situation you have had in the past.

221. How will you handle the stress of PA school?

222. What is the most stressful part of your current job?

223. What coping mechanisms have you developed for dealing with stress?

224. Tell me about a time you used teamwork to solve a problem.

225. Do you prefer to work with others or by yourself?

226. What is the most important factor between a PA and supervising physician?

227. Do you think it's more important to get patients seen or spend time with patients?

228. If a patient is late, should they still be seen?

229. How much time should be allotted to spend with each patient?

230. Describe your work ethic.

231. How are your time management skills?

232. Did you work while getting your prerequisites?

233. Would you say you're a hard worker?

234. What did you have to sacrifice to get to this interview?

235. Give an example of a goal you reached and tell how you achieved it.

236. Where do you get your motivation?

237. What would your best friend say about you?

238. Tell me about a situation when you had to push yourself.

239. Would you accept a Facebook friend request from a patient?

240. How has technology affected healthcare?

241. How do you predict technology will affect healthcare in the future?

242. Do you think providers should be Facebook friends with patients?

243. How would you feel in PA school if you were doing poorly in a subject that you excelled in during undergrad?

244. Do you ever get angry or frustrated?

245. How do you handle disappointment?

246. Define professionalism.

247. What does professionalism mean to you?

248. What does it mean to portray yourself in a professional manner?

249. Tell me about someone you've worked with who exhibited professionalism.

250. If you were to win the lottery, what would you do? Would you still want to be a PA?

251. Do you realize you'll make less money than a physician?

252. Should PAs be reimbursed at the same rate as physicians?

253. If PAs made $20,000 a year, would you still want to be a PA?

254. Give an example of a situation in which you exceeded expectations.

255. Tell me about a time that you surprised yourself.

256. Discuss a time that you had to help someone else out.

257. Tell me about a time you broke the rules.

258. What is the worst mistake you have ever made?

259. How has your interview experience been today?

260. Did you learn anything new about our program today?

261. What stood out to you most about your experience at the interview today?

262. Tell me about the last person who interviewed you.

263. What were the names of the interviewers you already met today?

264. Is there anything else I need to know about you?

265. Tell me something that's not on your application.

266. Tell me something you've never told anyone else.

267. If you had a memoir, what would it be called?

268. When you leave today what one thing will you wish you could have told us about yourself?

269. Discuss a current medical ethics issues.

270. Talk about a time you had to make an ethical decision.

271. Is it ethical to treat your family members? Would you do it?

272. If a patient has AIDS, will you still treat them?

273. You have diagnosed a patient with HIV, and they do not want to tell their partner. What do you do?

274. What would you do if you diagnose a patient with syphilis, but he doesn't plan to tell his girlfriend?

275. You are a PA. Your supervising MD asks you to administer a medication to a patient. You do not agree with his decision and feel it could harm the patient. What do you do?

276. You see a co-worker taking medication from the dispense cart and putting it in her bag. What do you do?

277. If you found out a classmate had old copies of exams, what would you do?

278. You are in a surgery and the anesthesiologist begins to make inappropriate comments about the patient once they are asleep. What do you do in this situation?

279. You're in an OR and have suspicions that the surgeon may be intoxicated. What do you do?

280. You have an elderly patient who needs to stay at the hospital for overnight observation. The patient is refusing, but the patient's son states the patient has dementia and is incapable of making medical decisions. The patient's son wants the patient admitted. What do you do?

281. You are leaving for the day and realize you gave a patient medication they are allergic to. What do you do?

282. A patient comes in for follow-up and you realize they were prescribed the wrong medication, but one with a similar name. What do you do?

283. You are working as a PA. You realize your nurse sent in the wrong medication for a patient. What do you do?

284. You realize you sent an adult dosage of medication for a child. What do you do?

285. You've prescribed an antibiotic, but after the patient leaves you realize there's a contraindication with one of their other medications. What do you do?

286. A patient calls back for their culture results, and you realize the test was never sent in. The sample is no longer good. What do you do?

287. When is honesty not the best policy?

288. You are seeing a Jehovah's Witness patient. Due to religious beliefs, he/she does not accept blood transfusions, but it could be life-saving. What do you do?

289. A child is brought in with injuries from falling out of a tree at a friend's house. His parents are out of town. After

evaluation, it is determined that he requires a blood transfusion. Before giving the transfusion, you find a card in his pocket stating he is Jehovah's Witness and to not give blood transfusions. The procedure would save his life, but no parents are present. What do you do?

290. You are a PA and you prescribed birth control pills for a 13-year-old. The patient's mother is angry about this decision. What do you say?

291. What would you do if you hit your neighbor's dog?

292. What would you do if you hit a car in a parking lot? You're unsure of the owner.

293. If you were a tree, what kind would you be and why?

294. If you were a color, what color would you be, and why?

295. If you were dressing up for a halloween party for kids, what would you dress up as, and why?

296. If you were a car, what kind would you be, and why?

297. If you were a candy bar, what kind would you be, and why?

298. If you could have any super power, what would you choose, and why?

299. If you were an animal, what would you be, and why?

300. What three people, living or dead, would you invite to dinner? What would you serve them?

301. Name three role models and why you look up to them.

302. What characteristics make a person a good role model?

303. If you could spend a day with one person, who would you choose, and why? What would you do?

304. What would you do if you were president for a day?

305. Help this student complete the following task...

306. Give directions for putting on a pair of gloves.

307. Give instructions for making a peanut butter and jelly sandwich.

308. While sitting back to back, tell the person in the room how to draw a tree.

309. Explain how to make a paper airplane.
310. Help the patient in the room fill out their intake form. (Once in the room, you find that the patient is homeless, cannot read, and does not know much of the information.)
311. Interpret the graph displayed in the room.
312. Enter the room and perform the following calculations...
313. Convert the medication amount from milligrams to grams.
314. Discuss a pastime outside of school and how the skills acquired will help in your career.
315. If you could have any other job, besides being a PA or working in the medical field, what would you do?
316. Discuss an experience that allowed you to learn something important about yourself.
317. What do you enjoy outside of work and school?
318. You are on the committee to hire a new faculty member for the PA program. What characteristics and/or qualities would you look for when selecting an effective teacher?
319. What are the 3 most important aspects in evaluating a PA program? What about a PA student?
320. What can our faculty do for you?
321. What accommodations will you need to successfully complete this program?
322. If you could do anything else and know you would be successful, what would you do?
323. Discuss a time you had to resolve a conflict.
324. Tell me about a time you worked with someone you didn't like.
325. Discuss a time you had to communicate effectively under pressure.
326. Talk about a time you had to disagree with someone to get a positive outcome.
327. What are you famous for?

328. What are you well known for?

329. Why do people recognize you?

330. You are caring for an obese patient on multiple medications, some of which are causing side effects. Would you recommend a change in medications or lifestyle?

331. You discover a classmate is romantically involved with her preceptor. What should be done, if anything? Enter the room and discuss your position.

332. What would you do if you saw a classmate cheating on an exam?

333. A friend in your class confides in you that his mother was recently diagnosed with breast cancer. He is overwhelmed and may drop out of school to spend time with his mother. How do you counsel your friend?

334. You are a dermatology PA. A patient states they are out of opioid pain medication and unable to get more from their pain management physician for another few weeks. What do you do?

335. You are seeing a patient who is a gymnast and currently training for the Olympics. The patient's mother is upset because the patient recently gained 3 pounds. Enter the room and address this situation.

336. A boat is sinking. There is a lifeboat for one person. The passengers include a 75-year-old physician, 50-year-old army officer, 24-year-old teacher, and a 6-year old. Who gets the spot?

SO WHAT'S NEXT?

Now that you've completed the book and have more knowledge about how to attack your interview, make sure you take plenty of time to practice. For more resources, visit www.thePAplatform.com. To stay up to date on current events in the PA field, join the monthly newsletter - www.thepaplatform.com/newsletter

If you enjoyed the book, and feel you gained valuable knowledge, I would be forever grateful if you would leave a review on Amazon to help other PA hopefuls know what they can look forward to.

Bulk orders of the book are available for Pre-PA Clubs at a discounted rate, and you can go to www.thepaplatform.com/book for more information.

If you've spent time practicing out loud, and still feel uncomfortable or want some professional feedback, I would encourage you to consider scheduling a Mock Interview through The PA Platform. All of our coaches are practicing PAs from various backgrounds and programs. You can use the code "book" at checkout for a discount when scheduling your service. Our mock interviews consist of 1 hour of coaching personalized to your upcoming interview style and written feedback. We've helped hundreds of applicants hone their interview skills to gain admission into PA school, and we would love to help you too! www.thepaplatform.com/mock-interview

Go forth and rock your interview! Fingers crossed, and I look forward to calling you my colleague in the future. As always, email The PA Platform with any questions at savanna@thepaplatform.com.

- Savanna

RESOURCES

THE PA PLATFORM

The PA Platform - For the best information out there for hopeful pre-PA students on the path to becoming physician assistants - http://www.thepaplatform.com

On The PA Platform website, you'll find blog posts, webinars, videos, and free downloads to help you feel as prepared as possible on your journey to PA school.

Make sure you're following along on social media for the most recent announcements:

- Instagram: @thePAplatform
- Facebook: http://www.facebook.com/thePAplatform
- Youtube: http://www.youtube.com/thePAplatform
- Pinterest: http://www.pinterest.com/thePAplatform
- Twitter: http://www.twiter.com/thePAplatform

THE PRE-PA CLUB PODCAST

For weekly podcast episodes, subscribe to The Pre-PA Club Podcast on iTunes, or visit http://www.thepaplatform.com/podcast to access all episodes. We frequently interview PAs and PA students, and you can even leave a voicemail question to have featured on the podcast.

THE PRE-PA CLUB FACEBOOK GROUP

The PA Platform, in collaboration with myPAresource, runs a Facebook group exclusive to Pre-PA students called "The Pre-PA Club." Make sure you join to gain access to a forum to ask questions and get feedback from practicing PAs and your peers.

INTERVIEW DATES

- Program:_____
- Date: _____
- Contact Person: _____
- Interview Information:

_____

- Program:_____
- Date: _____
- Contact Person: _____
- Interview Information:

_____

- Program:_____
- Date: _____
- Contact Person: _____
- Interview Information:

- Program:_____
- Date: _____
- Contact Person: _____
- Interview Information:

- Program:_____
- Date: _____
- Contact Person: _____
- Interview Information:

- Program:_____
- Date: _____
- Contact Person: _____
- Interview Information:

- Program:_____
- Date: _____
- Contact Person: _____
- Interview Information:

- Program:_____
- Date: _____
- Contact Person: _____
- Interview Information:

NOTES

Made in the USA
Middletown, DE
03 August 2020